Justice Nadeau is a graduate of Phillips Exeter Academy, Dartmouth College, and Boston University School of Law. He was appointed Associate Justice of the New Hampshire Superior Court in 1981 and served as Chief Justice of that court from 1991 until he was appointed an Associate Justice of the Supreme Court in 2000. He retired at the end of 2005 to continue twenty-five years of international judicial activities. He has participated in Rule of Law programs in Albania, Algeria, Armenia, Bulgaria, the Czech Republic, Egypt, Indonesia, Japan, Jordan, Kazakhstan, Latvia, Poland, Slovakia, the Soviet Union, and Ukraine.

Dedicated to the men and women everywhere who put country above self and who work tirelessly toward a community of nations.

JOSEPH NADEAU

AT HOME ABROAD:
FRIENDSHIP FIRST

A LOOK AT RULE OF LAW PROJECTS AND OTHER INTERNATIONAL INSIGHTS

AUSTIN MACAULEY PUBLISHERS™

LONDON • CAMBRIDGE • NEW YORK • SHARJAH

Copyright © Joseph Nadeau (2019)

Ordering Information:
Quantity sales: special discounts are available on quantity purchases by corporations, associations, and others. For details, contact the publisher at the address below.

Publisher's Cataloging-in Publication data
Nadeau, Joseph
At Home Abroad: Friendship First
A Look at Rule of Law Projects and Other International Insights

ISBN 9781641828727 (Paperback)
ISBN 9781641828734 (Hardback)
ISBN 9781641828741 (Kindle e-book)
ISBN 9781645366270 (ePub e-book)

Library of Congress Control Number: 2019935094

The main category of the book: LAW / Essays

www.austinmacauley.com/us

First Published (2019)
Austin Macauley Publishers LLC
40 Wall Street, 28th Floor
New York, NY 10005, USA

mail-usa@austinmacauley.com
+1 (646) 5125767

Thanks to my wife, Catherine, for her encouragement during the writing, collecting, and editing of the book. Thanks to our daughters, Tina, Diana, and Briana, for their suggestions and support.

A heartfelt appreciation to all the authors for their contribution to the book and for their work in the field.

And thanks to Dr. James Apple for his special contribution.

I would also like to acknowledge my friend and retired University of New Hampshire professor, Dr. James Jelmberg, who gave me the idea for this collection.

Preface

The inspiration for this book came from over twenty years of involvement in programs sponsored by the United States Agency for International Development (USAID), both as an American Bar Association (ABA) volunteer and after retirement, as a paid judicial specialist.

The authors of these chapters represent over two hundred years of international commitment to universal principles of justice, and their work has helped to promote an understanding of the importance of the rule of law and the independence of the judiciary. The unique perspective of each author is typical of the impact working internationally can have upon everyone involved. The experiences of each demonstrate that Americans working in other countries are not the only ones who are at home abroad.

As government leaders debate the role of the United States in international affairs, I hope this book will help to demonstrate why it is important to continue programs like those supported by USAID. With its successes and its challenges, promoting the rule of law at home and abroad is not an easy task. Cooperative efforts may take time to produce results, but they do have promise. People participating in these programs establish lasting relationships, promote mutual respect, and help to keep their nations at the forefront of international development.

I asked the American authors to write about their work in emerging democracies to highlight programs promoting rule of law principles. Most of us have spent our professional lives advocating for the principle of the rule of law at home and abroad. We all focused on fundamental concepts that form the basis of a healthy democracy; a free press, transparency in government, combatting corruption, separation of powers, equality of branches of government, and an independent judiciary.

When I began this project, I had no idea that these very principles might be at risk in our own country. Until now, I have never felt that we were in peril of losing our reputation as a shining example of how democratic institutions function.

Maybe the lessons we all learned from our international work will provide valuable assistance to those who labor not only to advance the rule of law, but to preserve it here as well.

So, for those who believe it useful to express a vision of any great country in simple slogans, I would like to suggest these:

The Rule of Law First.
Friendship First.
At home.
And abroad.

Joseph Nadeau
January 20, 2019

Foreword

United States Agency for International Development – Mission

USAID's efforts directly enhance American – and global – security and prosperity. The United States is safer and stronger when fewer people face destitution, when our trading partners are flourishing, when nations around the world can withstand crisis, and when societies are freer, more democratic, and more inclusive, protecting the basic rights and human dignity of all citizens. By focusing on these two goals, together, we position ourselves to meet the challenges of today while mitigating the risks of tomorrow.

(www.usaid.gov/who-we-are/mission-vision-values)

Council of Europe – Aims
To protect human rights, pluralist democracy and the rule of law;
To promote awareness and encourage the development of Europe's cultural identity and diversity;
To seek solutions to problems facing European society, such as: discrimination against minorities, xenophobia, intolerance, environmental protecting, human cloning, terrorism, human trafficking, organized crime and corruption, cybercrime, violence against children;
To help consolidate democratic stability in Europe by backing political, legislative, and constitutional reform.

(www.coe.int/en/web/sarajevo/objectives-mission)

Introduction

Medhat Al-Mahmood

Chief Justice Federal Supreme Court of Iraq

In my country, the history of judicial independence is still being written. Except in rare instances, the previous regime, which fell on April 9, 2003, deliberately isolated all segments of the Iraqi people, particularly the judiciary, from communication with, and knowledge of events in, the outside world. It did not permit Iraqi judges to leave Iraq to become acquainted with foreign judges, their ways of dealing with litigants and litigation, or even their protocols, culture, and environment. The previous regime feared that Iraqis who left the country would see what was going on in the world and realize that the regime was not allowing them to live – or even come close to living – a full, humane life.

I was appointed acting Minister of Justice on June 17, 2003. At that time, I sensed the isolation that Iraqis had endured as well as a desire and willingness on the part of international organizations to help Iraqis, particularly judges and public advocates (sometimes mistranslated as public prosecutors), become knowledgeable about the workings of foreign judiciaries. I conveyed this sense to the United States Agency for International Development (USAID) and the U.S. embassy in Baghdad.

Thereafter, we coordinated with the Higher Judicial Council to plan a project that would involve sending judicial delegations to the advanced countries and organizing activities in Iraq to improve the professionalism and performance of judges. Many organizations worked together on these initiatives. From 2003 to 2014, close to 1000 judges were sent on study missions abroad. This was an excellent experience for them. They may not have absorbed everything in Europe, America, or even the Arab states, but they were exposed to the experiences of foreign judiciaries and to judicial proceedings in the developed world.

In 2005, I took a delegation of senior judges to a program in Bratislava, Slovakia, conducted by CEELI of the American Bar Association. There I met and worked with Justice Nadeau and Mr. Zimmer to draft possible provisions in the new constitution that would help enhance the independence of the judiciary. Full independence like that in the U.S. is not yet possible in my country but we have been working toward that goal.

We continued this approach with the cooperation of international organizations, sending abroad many judges at the expense of those organizations, rather than at the expense of the Iraqi judiciary, as funding was not available for so many judges to travel abroad after the regime changed.

We take great pride in this experiment. It benefited our judiciary and the individuals who participated. It opened new horizons for us to develop our judicial activity based on what we learned in other developed countries. We previously lacked adequate knowledge about the judiciaries of the developed countries. To be sure, as an Arab expert in some legal fields, I was acquainted with the Egyptian and Jordanian judiciaries. However, those judiciaries are not on a par with the American and European judiciaries.

Broad paths and horizons were opened to me, as a judicial leader, to integrate, within the Iraqi judicial tradition, the experiences of others, particularly new ways for facilitating investigations and expediting decisions. I also became acquainted with the approaches of other judges in dealing with other parties, including lawyers. I can fairly say that the experience was unique and beneficial.

For example, I was able to become familiar with an experiment in California designed to train law students to become future judges, public prosecutors, and lawyers. I was very impressed to see a law student come before a court presided over by an experienced judge, prepare a pleading using pre-prepared forms, submit the pleading to the judge, and fully present the plaintiff's case. Upon my return to Iraq, I contacted the law schools and the Judicial Institute with a view toward replicating this experiment. However, I unfortunately encountered numerous obstacles, particularly the Bar Association's rejection of the initiative as it believed that it encroached on its work.

I also became familiar with legal clinics, which I found to be a splendid way to help citizens obtain legal assistance, particularly low-income women and minors. I promoted a legal clinic project for Iraq. Many organizations adopted it, including the USAID, which funded attractive salaries for lawyers to run legal clinics. I selected older, experienced lawyers to work in the clinics. This project unfortunately ended after its funding was depleted. It also encountered significant opposition from lawyers.

I still believe that joining conventions or treaties with international human rights organizations concerned with ensuring fair trials and tracking the cases of detainees is vitally important, and I encourage any initiative of this kind.

We have also been very interested in consolidating court procedures for hearing similar actions. We agreed with international organizations to designate certain courts as model courts and to apply to them a specific system, with the view toward applying the system to the other courts if it proved successful. A model court was designated near Rusafa in Baghdad. Others were designated in Kirkuk and in Basra. These efforts succeeded. We consolidated procedures in the court to ensure the speedy adjudication of actions and plaintiffs' easy obtainment of their rights at the lowest cost possible.

We continue to develop these programs and now have an excellent academic cadre that is developing Iraqi expertise in eliminating superfluous court procedures in coordination with the judges. This is one of the positive outcomes of our cooperation with international organizations. I can state with certainty that we have achieved 75 percent of the objectives set out for projects implemented by international organizations in Iraq.

These projects need time, training, and the faith of lawyers and judges in their feasibility. We have succeeded in helping young judges develop themselves but have had less success with older judges, which I also observed in Dubai, where older judges claim to use modern work methods but do not seem to be genuinely convinced to do so.

Regarding my current work, my time and efforts are divided between the Federal Supreme Court and the Higher Judicial Council. The Higher Judicial Council administers the affairs of judges and public advocates. However, the latter are only administratively subordinate to the Council, which does not interact with them, consistent with the principle of judicial independence.

I humbly believe that I have succeeded over the past 13 years in this work and achieved positive outcomes, including increasing the number of judges from 573 to 1,600. During this period, the palaces of justice (i.e., courthouses) have used modern methods and the courts have become linked to an electronic network, enabling them to transmit information within minutes. Concurrently, we established, in cooperation with the U.S. Government, an institute called the Judicial Development Institute, which offers all judges courses lasting 7 to 10 days. No judge or public advocates may be promoted without passing one or two of the institute's courses.

Regardless of whether I remain or after I am succeeded, I continue to believe in the need to further strengthen the judiciary in all respects and to apply the principle of the separation of powers without neglecting the principle of cooperation between the powers. We, therefore, experimented – successfully I believe – by forming judicial investigation offices. These offices directly receive and decide legal actions brought to it by citizens, who need not go through the police stations, which fall under the executive authority. The staffs of these offices may include one or more judicial magistrates, public advocates, and judicial investigators, depending on the workload.

I believe that these offices have been successful despite the police agencies' unspoken but significant opposition to and obstruction of their work. We are determined to support and increase the number of such offices. We call upon the developed nations to assist us in training investigators and judicial magistrates in the use of up-to-date investigation methods. In this regard, we initially sought the assistance of foreign experts. However, we found that not everything abroad is suitable for our purposes in creating a model. We have therefore blended the Iraqi judicial tradition with foreign developments.

We now prepare programs using Iraqi personnel, experts, and concepts, in addition to advanced foreign expertise. We are self-reliant in our program design capacity and have a department comprising 130 specialists for this purpose.

Our mission to improve the Iraqi judiciary and retake its proper place in history is unwavering. We acknowledge and appreciate the assistance we received from international organizations and friendly countries over the years and look forward to future opportunities for further cooperation.

Chief Justice Medhat (center) with NH Supreme Court Justices (from left) Galway, Nadeau, CJ Broderick, and Duggan.

Chief Justice Mahmoud addresses the NH Supreme Court after receiving the Supreme Court Society's first 'Life and Liberty Award'.

Contents

Chapter 1
Beginnings
Attorney Mary Noel Pepys

A golden bore. That's how I described my life in 1993 as an attorney with a thriving land use practice, a gorgeous view of San Francisco Bay from my home, weekend jaunts to Napa Valley, weekday tennis games, and a local culinary and cultural scene that is the envy of many. A golden life, to be sure, but I was bored.

Having watched with utter fascination, the dismantling of the Berlin Wall, signifying the demise of communism, I wanted to be where the political action was. I wanted to help in the creation of constitutions for the recently liberated republics of the former Soviet Union and for the newly independent central and eastern European countries. I wanted to assist in the drafting of laws, which embraced democratic values and market-based economic principles.

Thanks to two American visionary attorneys, Sandy D'Alemberte and Homer Moyer, a new program was founded by the American Bar Association, ABA ROLI (Rule of Law Initiative, formerly Central and Eastern European Law Initiative, and later Central European and Eurasian Law Initiative). The mission of ABA ROLI, which is funded primarily by USAID, is to promote justice, economic opportunity and human dignity through the rule of law.

At the time of its inception, ABA ROLI had a small staff at its Washington D.C. headquarters and an even smaller group of willing American attorneys who worked *pro bono* throughout central and Eastern Europe, and the former Soviet Union, to engage in developing the rule of law in these former communist ruled countries.

In the fall of 1993, I succumbed to the unknown and boarded a plane for Sofia, Bulgaria, where I agreed to volunteer with ABA ROLI for six months, to provide legal assistance to enhance Bulgaria's judicial system, legal profession, and its legal educational system. Not only were Bulgaria's constitution and laws in need of an overhaul, but also the habit of legal professionals, particularly judges, of yielding to the whims of communist party leaders had to be curtailed. Additionally, the attitude of Bulgarians who were accustomed to State subsidies of housing, food, employment, medical care, and vacations needed a radical change. No longer would the State be responsible for such subsidies. Bulgarians, like their former communist neighbors, had to assume the obligation of freedom, taking responsibility for their own lives.

After settling into my assigned apartment, located in a crumbling utilitarian apartment building, that was surrounded by a dozen identically unattractive buildings, with no heat, despite the freezing temperature (the central heating system was still controlled by the government), little hot water, and darkened hallways (light bulbs were stolen by the other residents), I began my work with the idealistic enthusiasm of a 1960s peace corps volunteer.

But unlike most Peace Corps volunteers, I was inexperienced in the area in which I was to help. Developing the rule of law was a nascent endeavor for Americans. In fact, the term 'rule of law' was not only foreign to citizens of former communist countries, but also to most Americans. Today, however, it has been incorporated into the lexicon in describing a country's governmental system. According to the United Nations, "The rule of law as a concept refers to a principle of governance in which all persons, institutions and entities, public and private, including the state itself, are accountable to laws that are publicly promulgated, equally enforced and independently adjudicated, and which are consistent with international human rights norms and standards."

Other than USAID's promotion of democracy in Latin America in the 1980's, few American attorneys had the opportunity to engage in rule of law work. Thus, while those of us who volunteered for ABA ROLI in the early 90s had significant legal experience, we were novices in developing the rule of law. What set us apart, however, was that we all shared a common vision and a desire to participate in the birthing process of democracy. We were willing to travel paths unchartered and to endure hardships that were still commonplace in countries transitioning from communism.

Our only direction from ABA ROLI was to 'go forth and do good' as there were no contractual statements of work or annual work plans. We did not have monitoring and evaluation flowcharts, nor time-consuming reporting requirements. We had few demands and limitations placed upon us and were able to chart our own course. Our work plan, so to speak, emanated from the expressed needs of the people. This was manna to ABA ROLI volunteers, like myself, who were accustomed in their legal career to taking charge.

Under these circumstances, everything was possible. We could meet with anyone *we* wanted and respond quickly to any type of legal assistance *they* wanted. We were not hindered by a predetermined set of goals. We were left to our own devices, and those of us who were self-starters, flourished, limited only by our lack of initiative and imagination.

It was a magical time. The spirit of volunteerism, rather than a paycheck, inspired us. I remember well a telephone conversation I had with an ABA ROLI volunteer in Macedonia in 1994, who was awake at 3:00 a.m., as I was, discussing with excitement the ideas we wanted to pursue the following day. We joked with each other that we had no personal life. No wonder we were still single.

At that time, ABA ROLI was the only game in town and everyone in the legal community of the countries we served sought us out. There was no duplication of efforts by other organizations; there was no tripping over other consultants with competing or overlapping projects from American contractors and European entities. In fact, at the time I was in Bulgaria, there was just a handful of American attorneys helping to enhance democratic reforms in Bulgaria.

The early 90s were euphoric and everyone had high expectations and eagerness to pursue democratic reforms. Each day in Bulgaria was a new day of exploration, of meeting anyone who demonstrated an interest in rule of law reform, of responding quickly to their various requests, of being creative in designing solutions to meet their needs, and of forging ahead without fixed expectations or restrictions.

While most governmental officials were eager to seek democratic changes, some were not. Developing a constitutional government with genuine separation of powers resulted in the eventual reduction or elimination of the power of certain governmental officials who, heretofore, had significant power and were reluctant to support such reforms. I encountered this reaction first-hand in Bulgaria.

In those days, the development protocol, such as it was, was a top-down approach. Thus, it was essential to discuss initially with the Ministry of Justice, particularly the Minister, ABA ROLI's interest in supporting judicial reforms. I made numerous attempts to meet with the Minister, twice arriving at his office at the scheduled time, confronting an empty chair behind his desk. There was speculation regarding the Minister's failed promises to meet with me, many believing he was anti-American which was not uncommon among other bureaucrats I met, or wanted to hold on to his days of glory under the old regime, as his staff surmised.

Thus, I had to devise another route to pursue judicial reforms. I switched to the bottom-up grassroots approach by reaching out to individual judges, not only those in Sofia, but also in other towns far from the capital's central government, where citizens were more accustomed to speak and act freely.

With my new approach, I met four Bulgarian women judges, two from Sofia and two from Varna, a beautiful coastal town on the Black Sea, who were eager to implement democratic reforms in Bulgaria. As ABA ROLI had not imposed a precise activity that I was required to pursue with these judges, I spent considerable time with them, ascertaining *their* needs and how ABA ROLI could respond to *their* priorities. We had numerous meetings, which I regularly ended with a list of next steps for each of us to complete. And yet, although they were interested in pursuing reforms, they accomplished little between meetings, while I, a typical American attorney, was eagerly checking off each item on the list for which I was responsible. Little did I know they were testing me. Was it worth their time to take the next steps? Could they trust me? Was I genuinely interested in helping them?

After numerous weeks of frustrating perseverance, I was thrilled to learn that they ultimately decided that it was worth their time to spend with me. Together, we decided that ABA ROLI could help create a legal training center that would train prospective prosecutors and judges, as well as provide continuing legal education of current prosecutors and judges. Unlike common law countries where highly experienced lawyers are appointed or elected to the bench, most judges in civil law countries are assigned to the bench shortly after law school.

Consequently, a continuing legal education program is necessary in civil law countries to focus on building the prosecutorial and judicial skills of future jurists. Although I had no mandate or even suggestion by ABA ROLI or USAID to create a legal training center, both ABA ROLI and USAID were enthusiastically supportive of my efforts, given that the need for it emanated from the Bulgarians.

After several months of working closely together, the four women judges drafted by-laws and the initial curriculum for a non-profit legal training center they wanted to create. While appreciating my grassroots approach in pursuing judicial reforms, the judges were well aware of the necessity for the Minister of Justice and the Prosecutor General to support their concept of a legal training center. On their own initiative, they strategized to obtain governmental approval and were eventually successful.

As luck would have it, we learned that Chief Justice William Rehnquist would be visiting Bulgaria at the same time we were pursuing national support for the legal training center. *Surely, the most important jurist in the U.S. would be interested in the plight of Bulgarian judges,* I thought. With unabashed naiveté, I approached U.S. Ambassador William P. Montgomery with a request that the U.S. Embassy invite Chief Justice Rehnquist to speak at a judges' seminar in Varna to support the legal training center. He rolled his eyes upward thinking I had gone mad.

But, the four judges and I were determined, and with the ultimate help of the U.S. Embassy and ABA ROLI, Chief Justice Rehnquist was invited and accepted our invitation. We met in Sofia and together with his staff and U.S. government personnel, flew to Varna. During the seminar, he experienced some comic relief when an embarrassed participant reflexively referred to other judges as his 'comrades' rather than colleagues. It had only been a few years since that label was *de rigueur*. Habits die slowly. Due to the intense national publicity surrounding his visit, judges throughout Bulgaria were inspired to join our efforts to create the legal training center, which the four judges called Legal Initiative for Training and Development, PIOR (Cyrillic acronym).

With legal documents in hand, but no funding for PIOR, the four judges and I began a fundraising campaign. Knowing of potential funds at the U.S. Embassy through its Democracy Commission, we met with U.S. Ambassador Montgomery to seek funding. The judges were powerful advocates, and after a convincing presentation, PIOR received $25,000 from the Democracy Commission for its start-up costs. This was a significant amount in the early 90s that had a serious impact in creating PIOR. For several years thereafter, due to the judges' fundraising efforts, PIOR survived on donor support in conducting numerous seminars and workshops, and international conferences.

Recognizing that judicial training must be government-funded in order to be sustainable, the Bulgarian government, with the support of USAID, created the National Institute of Justice (NIH) in 2004, which assumed the role of PIOR. While PIOR no longer exists, the four women judges continue to thrive in the legal and judicial communities of Bulgaria. Last year, one of them became the Executive Director of the NIH, capitalizing upon her experience in developing PIOR. Prior to that, she had been appointed as the Minister of Justice. One judge served in the European Parliament, while another ran for the Vice Presidency of Bulgaria, and the fourth was promoted to the Supreme Court of Cassation of Bulgaria.

In essence, PIOR was created without an institutional mandate but, instead, with individual initiative. Four Bulgarian judges, one American attorney, and local staff attorneys began their work together without any contractual direction or funding. Yet, because of their shared commitment to meet the needs of Bulgarian judges, their energetic engagement in the development process, the political will of the Ministry of

Justice and the Prosecutor General of Bulgaria, and the financial support of ABA ROLI, USAID, and the U.S. Embassy, an essential reform in the judicial system of Bulgaria was created.

In conjunction with working on judicial reform also helped strengthen the Bulgarian Bar Association (BBA), which later became an essential component of ABA ROLI's assistance in Bulgaria in the mid-90s. Banned by communist rule after WWII in 1945, the BBA, which was created in 1923, was reinstated in 1991 with a membership of 4,000 attorneys.

During one of my first meetings with the President of the BBA, he proudly showed me a fledgling four-page newsletter on flimsy paper that the BBA sent to the offices of the 28 district bar associations. It was startling to see such primitive resources in an important national organization headed by a very intelligent attorney. But it was all the BBA could afford. The President wanted to increase the quality of the articles of the newsletter and to circulate it directly to every member, so that the BBA could become a leader in enhancing democracy and the independence of the judiciary.

We held meetings with other members of the BBA who were eager to improve the newsletter by writing their own articles on developing a legal profession for private practitioners. They wanted the BBA newsletter to educate all attorneys about the private practice of law, particularly law practice management, client relations, and billing. It was not an easy task to have meetings with them as their offices took a treasure hunt map to find, cubbyholes located down long, darkened corridors in buildings with rickety stairwells and uneven steps. Prohibited under the former regime to join together as a law firm, most attorneys practiced solo for years with modest income. That has changed considerably since 1993. Today, numerous law firms exist in Bulgaria occupying premises that rival law firms around the world.

After meetings with several, highly engaged and energetic attorneys, it did not take long to be convinced of their commitment to reform. With the continued flexibility to assist in any way I thought appropriate, I approached, once again, the U.S. Embassy for funding. As a result, the BBA received

$8,000 from the Democracy Commission that was sufficient to meet the publication goals of the BBA.

Engaging in a rule of law project was straightforward in those days. And the process for each rule of law practitioner was similar. We ascertained a local need, designed a project to meet the need, obtained political will for the project, engaged locally committed and highly skilled professionals to implement the project, and supported it with international technical assistance and funding.

Concurrently with helping to create PIOR and to develop the BBA newsletter, I was free to meet with anyone else who wanted assistance. Law professors who wanted American legal texts translated into Bulgarian; city planning bureaucrats who were keen on developing privatization laws; parliamentarians who needed law drafting assistance; and lawyers who wanted to learn about commercial laws are just a sample of the disparate requests and welcomed meetings I had. This was all in a day's work, and each day the requests and meetings varied.

What was steady, however, was ABA ROLI's assistance. Since much of the assistance requested by the Bulgarians required expert opinions, ABA ROLI would provide substantive information that I could use as a rapid response. I remember being asked by a governmental official with the Ministry of Education for U.S. law school accreditation standards which he wanted me to present in a radio interview the following day. Without hesitation, ABA ROLI was able to draw upon the expertise of a nationally acclaimed law professor and provided me the necessary information in time for the radio interview. This was one of ABA ROLI's major strengths as it was able to turn to the entire membership of the ABA to provide advice and guidance *pro bono.*

A project I so enjoyed in Bulgaria was borne out of a meeting with a Bulgarian law professor who had recently visited the U.S. She was a professor at the New Bulgarian University School of Law, which was an alternative to the state-run Sofia University Law School and was founded in 1991 to provide creative opportunities for its law students. Having learned of law reviews in the US, she wanted to create a law review for the students of New Bulgarian University

School of Law. Law reviews, written and edited solely by law students, were a foreign concept in Bulgaria.

Why, law students asked, would legal experts, including attorneys and judges, read a scholarly article by a student who was just learning the law? Doesn't that smack of elitism by unqualified students, they questioned? Lacking self-confidence and fearing the prospect of failure, these law students were intimidated by a writing competition as they were not only accustomed to oral exams, but also uncomfortable with excelling over others having lived under the Soviet system where everyone was deemed equal. However, they forged ahead with the writing assignment and the winners began drafting their articles for the first student law review in Bulgaria.

Although ABA ROLI's *pro bono* work had a daunting impact on my finances, it became my passion. I extended my six-month commitment to one year in Bulgaria and then continued with ABA ROLI by working a year in Latvia, followed by a year in Slovakia, and the subsequent two years in Ukraine, Kazakhstan, and Croatia, for a total of five years. Had my work in Bulgaria not been as fruitful as it was, had the Bulgarian legal professionals not been as receptive and eager to pursue democratic reforms as they were; and had we not been as successful as we were, I doubt I would have found my passion.

Having cut my teeth on developing the rule of law in Bulgaria, I moved to Latvia in 1995 with a keener sense of my responsibilities and the challenges I would undoubtedly face. Starting with the living conditions, which I knew were not going to resemble the comforts of home, I rented an apartment formerly occupied by a high-level Russian soldier, whose living room chairs were still covered with fabric that proudly displayed the hammer and sickle. During winter, of all seasons, the hot water was turned off for several weeks to clean the pipes. Every morning, I would put two big pots of water on the stove to heat for a sponge bath, and while it was heating, I would take my garbage out to the apartment courtyard, to wait in a long line for the garbage truck to arrive so each of us tenants could place our garbage in the back of the garbage truck. This was my morning ritual.

While Latvia became independent around the same time as Bulgaria, the essential factors in developing a self-sustaining rule of law project were present in Latvia. My ABA ROLI predecessor had responded to the needs expressed by Latvian judges for a judicial training center, and by the time I arrived, had developed a consensus among key judges, including the Chief Justice of the Latvian Supreme Court, to create the Latvian Judicial Training Center (LJTC).

Relying upon the judges' support as a foundation, she orchestrated a national conference on judicial independence attended not only by judges and attorneys, but also parliamentarians and press, to stimulate government support and a public understanding of the need for an institution to train judges. In essence, with this one conference, the motivation was developed for the Latvians to take ownership of judicial reforms, and as a result, the legal and judicial communities supported the creation of the LJTC.

My predecessor and I overlapped, so that the continuation of ABA ROLI assistance to the judges in creating the LJTC was seamless. Since the underpinnings of the LJTC were solid due to her assistance in generating the foundational documents, I spent the majority of my year in Latvia working with its leadership to develop the LJTC. The first meeting of the Board of Directors of the LJTC, which I was fortunate to attend was eye opening, for it provided me insight into the Soviet style of governance. Remnants of the past, the Chair of the Board, while well-meaning, was autocratic, giving short-shrift to the opinions of the others, particularly if they were at variance with his own. He believed in the absolute power of the leader and was unaccustomed to democratic decision-making. In fact, it was obvious that ABA ROLI's assistance would be ineffective if we only focused on the services of the LJTC; we had to help democratize the organization and leadership of the LJTC.

Also revealing was the membership of the Board, another remnant of the past, which consisted of older judges and only one woman judge. This was at a time when 80% of the judiciary was women and an equal percentage young. ABA ROLI helped to inspire the Board's leadership to change its membership to reflect the composition of the judiciary, which ultimately took place after much resistance by young women judges who did not want to waste their time being marginalized by the other members of the Board.

One of the first tasks of the Board of the LJTC was to hire an Executive Director. Interestingly, the strongest candidate was a law student who represented the future, who was not accustomed to the restraints imposed by the Soviet system, and who had an uncanny ability to foresee issues that would typically arise from creating a non-governmental organization (NGO). While I was providing advice and guidance to her in developing the LJTC, it always seemed like she was a step ahead of me.

She, along with the Chair of the Board, and I spent hundreds of hours together for an entire year to establish the LJTC which became, in just one year, a nationally respected NGO. All of my work with the LJTC was at the behest of the Chair and the Executive Director, rather than in response to a set of responsibilities set forth by ABA ROLI. This was *the* crucial element of the LJTC's success. As with Bulgarians, I provided advice and guidance, while the local lawyers and judges engaged in the work.

While practitioners have a significant role in the progress of a rule of law project, one of the guarantees of its success is often the result of higher-level donor representatives participating in the development of the project. The American assistance to the LJTC was a collective effort, with strong support not only from USAID and ABA ROLI, but also the U.S. Embassy. U.S. Ambassador Larry Napper provided a Democracy Commission grant of $24,000 for the publication of legal documents by the LJTC, and attended various functions of the LJTC demonstrating America's commitment to democratic reforms in Latvia. While his wife, Mary, conducted English language courses at the LJTC, which became some of the most popular ones. Their combined efforts gave international credibility to the LJTC. "The U.S. Embassy and other foreign embassies' involvement in judicial reform efforts in Latvia was extraordinarily helpful, in that it demonstrated the importance of such reforms to the politicians and press," stated a Latvian attorney.

The support by U.S. Ambassador Napper for the work ABA ROLI engaged in with the LJTC in Latvia mirrored the support ABA ROLI received in Bulgaria for PIOR under U.S. Ambassador Montgomery. Had these two U.S. Ambassadors stayed on the sidelines during that crucial time of high receptivity for initiating the rule of law, I am certain the creation of PIOR and the LJTC would have been significantly hindered.

My international work up to now, was anything but boring. Following my five years working *pro bono* with ABA ROLI, I returned to San Francisco and continued my rule of law work as a consultant. I was hooked.

Atty Mary Noel Pepys with a group of international judges.

Chapter 2

Revival from a "Burnt-Out Case" Leads to International Law and an International Judicial Academy

Attorney James G. Apple

By the near end of the last century, I was a burned-out trial lawyer. I had entered law practice in the early 1960s, and except for military service and a two-year stint in state government, I had continually been engaged in the trial of civil cases, handling commercial cases, admiralty cases, personal injury cases, medical malpractice cases, and other types of civil cases that had found their way into the trial courts of Kentucky where I had settled. But as the 20th century wound down, I was becoming increasingly unhappy with law practice. My firm, which I had joined when it had only 19 lawyers, had become large (150+ lawyers spread out in five different geographical locations). I was only a statistic on the firm's monthly financial sheet that reported on, among other items, that hated number – the one for 'billable hours'. I had little contact with other partners. Outside lawyers with whom I had to deal had become increasingly uncivil. Finally, in 1988, I decided I had had enough.

But there was a problem: what could I do as an alternative? I still had college tuition to pay for one of my children, I wasn't interested in a business career, and I was too old (age 51) to prepare myself for another profession. There didn't seem to be any path to an alternative profession or occupation. Then, one afternoon, in the fall of 1987, when I was browsing through a legal magazine, I came upon a small advertizement for graduate law students to study international law abroad.

That ad was a spark that ignited a small flame inside me. Two of my occasional dreams had been, for a number of years,

(1) to study international law and (2) to study in the United Kingdom. I did some research about international law programs abroad for graduate students seeking a Master of Laws (LL.M.) degree. I also read over the partnership agreement that held my firm together and found a clause that allowed for partners to take sabbatical leave with partial pay. I made a decision: apply to the law firm for a sabbatical and apply for admission to several law schools in the U.K.

My request for a sabbatical with partial pay was granted, and I was accepted into the LL.M. program of the University of Edinburgh Faculty of Law (now University of Edinburgh Law School) in Scotland. I was energized by the feeling that I could find for myself another more meaningful life and place in the world.

Living in Edinburgh, attending a law school that had been teaching law since the 16th century, and experiencing Scottish culture 'up close and personal' turned out to be one of the great experiences of my life. It was a wonderful year, with stimulating classes during the week and tours around Scotland to visit the many local castles and gardens on the weekends. I will try to tell you how that year 'restored my soul'.

There were three follow-up experiences that signaled that I had made the right new career choice. The first was an epiphanic experience in the law school library one afternoon in the spring of 1989. I was browsing among the stacks, looking at the broad array of book titles on the shelves dealing with international law. There seemed to be an endless number of them. I thought: *There is a large gap between the international law in the many tomes surrounding me and the place, or non-place, for international law in the real world. International law seemed to be largely an academic exercise, confined to law libraries and law school lecture halls, with little or no relevance to or significance for the outside world, without impact on how people and nations acted toward each other.* I decided then and there that I would devote the remainder of my life to international law and strive to make it relevant 'in the market place', to make it a genuine force for peace and good in the world.

A second experience that was meaningful in my pursuit of a new vocation, grew out of an assignment in one of my classes to write an essay about a particular subject relating to public international law. I decided that the subject of my paper would be a study of the doctrine of self-defense in international humanitarian law (law of war). Coincidentally, during that academic year, the British Red Cross had announced an essay contest open to students at British universities for best paper in international humanitarian law. One of my professors urged me to enter my essay in the Red Cross contest. I refined my paper and submitted it to the Red Cross office in London. Other contestants included students from Oxford, Cambridge, and the University of London. An eminent English law professor and several distinguished British military officers were the judges for the contest.

After I had graduated from Edinburgh University with an LL.M. degree and returned home in the fall of 1989, I received a letter from the general counsel of the British Red Cross, advising that my essay had been awarded first prize in the contest. The prize was an all-expense paid trip for a short residency at the Henri Dunant Institute in Geneva, Switzerland, and another short residency at the Institute of International Humanitarian Law in San Remo, Italy.

When I embarked on my journey to the U.K. the year before, I was uncertain whether I could compete in the world I was entering, since my background in international law was very limited. Also, I had been away from academe for many years. The essay prize gave me confidence that I could succeed 'in the big time' of the new world I had chosen.

The third consequence of my study in Edinburgh (and winning the essay contest and visiting Geneva and San Remo) was that, within one year of my return to the U.S. I found a position at the Federal Judicial Center (FJC), the federal courts agency for education, training, and research, located in Washington, D.C. I was first Special Assistant to the Director, but was eventually put in charge of the international programs of the Center, a position for which my experience in Scotland and the University of Edinburgh proved invaluable. I stayed with the Judicial Center for nine and one-half years, until I left the Center to found the International Judicial Academy in the fall of 1999.

The time at the Center was the time when I really became immersed in international assistance programs and started several programs there relating to the work of judges and court administrators from other countries. The first was a Visiting Foreign Judicial Fellows Program that brought judges and jurists from other countries to be in residence at the Judicial Center for one to five months, to study and write a paper on a selected topic relating to judges and courts. That program is still popular at the FJC. Since its beginning, the Center has hosted 107 judges and jurists from courts and legal institutions around the world.

When I first arrived at the FJC in May 1990, there were very few international programs. The Center provided occasional briefings for visiting jurists and small delegations of visiting professionals from time to time, but there was no structure or guidelines for the conduct of such programs and no mechanism for letting the world know about the FJC and its work. However, that situation changed very soon after my arrival. The Soviet Union was breaking up. Russia and its former satellites had little or no experience in establishing a functioning, professionally staffed legal and court system. The United States stood ready to help.

One day in the fall of 1991, the then Director of the Center, Judge William W Schwarzer, from the U.S. District Court for the Northern District of California in San Francisco, received an invitation to lunch from the Undersecretary of State for Human Rights and Humanitarian Affairs in the U.S. State Department. He wanted to discuss how the Judicial Center could assist in providing educational programs for judges and court officers from Russia and the new independent states of the former Soviet Union.

During the lunch, he commented on the reason for his interest and request – he had finally realized, in his position relating to human rights, that "there could be no true protection of human rights without an independent judiciary". From that lunch, the FJC, working with the U.S. State Department, put together a three-week seminar on judicial and court related subjects in Washington for a group that included two judges each from Russia and the new independent states. Approximately 26 judges attended the seminar. That seminar marked for me the beginning of my involvement in international law-related assistance programs, continuous since that time for 25 years.

In my position as Chief of the Interjudicial Affairs Office, I was able to plan and conduct, with colleagues from the FJC and the Administrative Office of the U.S. Courts (AOUSC – which was in the same building), many additional seminars for groups of judges from different countries. One special series of programs was designed to assist judges and court officers from the Russian Federation. They resulted in the training of over 225 Russian judges to help create in their country modern legal and court systems. As a result of our experience with these series, we trained over 225 judges to help create modern and legal systems in their own countries.

The experience with the Russian judges resulted in two memorable occasions, serious when they happened, but humorous now on reflection. During one program involving both Russian judges and Russian prosecutors, there was a Russian prosecutor who happened to be working with the U.S. Federal Bureau of Investigation (FBI) on an international criminal matter which had repercussions both in the U.S. and Russian Federation. When the group was in Washington, an FBI agent from New York, working on the international criminal matter, expressed a desire to meet with a Russian prosecutor who was working on the same case and a member of the Russian delegation.

Plans were made for the New York FBI agent to come to Washington for the meeting. However, the New York FBI agent later advised his Washington colleagues that his pregnant wife was soon expected to deliver her child and he had to remain in New York to be with her. Plans were then made for the Russian prosecutor to travel by train to New York for the meeting.

There was one problem with the plan – the Russian prosecutor did not speak English and would thus not know when to get off the train. The Washington FBI agents advised how to solve the problem – when the train conductor walked through the train cars, he would be announcing the arrival in New York. The conductor announcement would be the signal for the Russian prosecutor to get off the train.

The Russian prosecutor left on the train for New York, and two New York agents were dispatched to meet him at New York's Pennsylvania Station. Hours later, the Washington agents received an urgent call from the two agents at Penn Station, who advised that the train had arrived without the Russian prosecutor. Panic ensued. The Washington FBI group realized that the Russian guest was now lost in the environs of New York or at least somewhere beyond Washington. An international incident was developing.

Finally, one of the Washington agents familiar with the Washington-New York train schedule figured out what probably had gone wrong. One of the last train stops along the Washington-New York route before reaching Pennsylvania Station is Newark, New Jersey. The Russian prosecutor had probably heard the conductor going through the train announcing "Newark, next stop". To the Russian's unfamiliar ear, the conductor sounded as if he were announcing 'New York'. The Russian prosecutor had probably gotten off the train at Newark.

The Washington agents immediately called the two agents waiting at Penn Station and told them to rush to the Newark train station. The two New York agents then left Penn Station, retrieved their car, and sped across the Hudson River and through the streets of Newark to the train station there. Fortunately, they soon found the stranded Russian prosecutor, who had had the presence of mind to remain at the Newark train station after disembarking from the train there. Thus, potential international incident was happily avoided.

The second incident involving Russian judges occurred during another Washington seminar. Two Russian judges, who were members of the delegation, informed my colleague, who had arranged for their hotel accommodations, that they were planning a visit to a friend who was a member of the Russian Embassy staff.

The two judges left early one evening by cab to the Russian diplomat's home in suburban Washington. When they arrived, the diplomat advised them that he and his wife had to attend a reception. They invited the two judges to stay in their home with the couples' teenage daughter until they returned later in the evening. Soon after they left, the daughter advised the two guests that she was leaving to visit a school friend who lived in the neighborhood.

Unbeknownst to her parents, who had not been advised about the visit, the daughter planned to spend the night at her friend's house, and she did not so advise the two judges. After she left, the judges waited for several hours for the parents to return. When they did not, the two judges left the house to return to their hotel in downtown Washington.

The diplomat and his wife were late returning to their home – in fact after midnight. Upon arriving at their house, they discovered their daughter missing and no visiting judges in the house. They assumed the worst, that their daughter had been kidnapped, and immediately called the security office of the U.S. State Department. This action launched a manhunt for the daughter and the two judges.

The State Department security officers eventually traced the judges to the IJA program and my colleague, who advised the name of the hotel where the Russian judges were staying.

These officers arrived at the hotel, explained to the hotel officials the circumstances of their arrival, and were allowed to go to the two judges' hotel room. Upon arrival at the door, they pounded on it and woke the two judges. When the door was opened, they took the two judges into custody to interrogate them about the missing daughter of the Russian diplomat.

Meanwhile, as morning was approaching, the diplomat's daughter decided to return home from the night at her friend's house. When she arrived there, to the great relief of her parents, they immediately called the U.S. State Department and advised that the wayward daughter had been located and was safe and sound at home. The security officers were notified, the judges were returned to their hotel room, undoubtedly completely confounded and upset at this unexpected turn of events. But another potential international incident had been avoided.

The total number of seminars that I planned and conducted over an eight-year period at the Center exceeded 50. I also conducted short briefings at the FJC for many other judges and jurists, hundreds in number during that same time period. I left the Center in the fall of 1999, since I was eligible for retirement and I wanted to develop a private, independent organization that would provide educational programs for judges and court officers from other countries on a full-time basis.

A former colleague from the AOUSC and I started the International Judicial Academy on $300. When I had the idea for an academy, I had decided that it would be a non-profit organization and that I would not receive from it any salary or remuneration. Fortunately, my financial situation allowed me, with the exception of two years, to abide by the decision to forgo any pay for my work. The Academy opened for business on October 1, 1999 after it had been chartered by the District of Columbia.

The idea for such an academy had been in the back of my mind for several years. I was aware of the National Judicial College in Reno, Nevada, which provides educational programs primarily for state judges. It occurred to me that there was need for a similar institution to provide education programs for judges, court officers, and rule of law officials from other countries, especially those from emerging nations, to help them build modern, fair, independent, transparent, efficient, and accessible court systems, with well-trained judges and court administrators. That would become the consistent mission of the IJA during its 17 years of existence.

A recent review and accounting of the work of the IJA during those 17 years revealed that it had conducted over 150 seminars and conferences on a variety of topics relating to the building of strong judiciaries and court systems; involving over 4,500 judges, court officers, government officials, and rule of law officials from over 15 countries around the world; including Russia, China, Brazil, Argentina, Chile, Romania, Egypt, Jordan, Morocco, Libya, Tunisia, Turkey, Liberia, and others. That record in and of itself has been a source of great satisfaction to me, and hopefully to the persons who have assisted in the work of the Academy, and those who have participated in its programs.

One program in which the Academy was involved was exciting during its conduct, but disappointing in the end. The Academy teamed with one of the large international program providers in Washington to conduct for the U.S. State Department a series of educational programs for judges in five MENA (Middle East North Africa) countries – Jordan, Egypt,

Morocco, Libya, and Tunisia. The IJA developed a three-week program in Washington for judges from those countries, followed months later by two short three-day conferences in Casablanca, Morocco. The educational programs went well, and the participating judges were on the cusp of creating a multi-country regional organization that would work for and support coordinated judicial reform efforts in all five countries. Only a few months after the second conference ended, two of the countries, Libya and Tunisia, experienced terrorist attacks, resulting in continued violence and the collapse of the judicial reform program that had been so meticulously planned.

Not only did the International Judicial Academy plan and conduct programs for judges, court officers, and rule of law officials from other countries, it provided one program for state and federal judges from the United States. This was the educational activity that I enjoyed most, but it also had a sad ending.

My interest in international law, whetted by one year living in Scotland, increased during my years at the Federal Judicial Center and then at the Academy.

I knew from my experience in associating with state and federal judges that many of them, maybe even most of them, knew very little, if anything, about international law and international courts. I had been to The Hague in the Netherlands on several occasions and developed the idea of a seminar in that Dutch city for state and federal judges on these two topics.

I secured some financial assistance from a foundation in New York, and then, in 2005, conducted in The Hague the first Sir Richard May Seminar on International Law and International Courts. The seminar was named after Judge Richard May, a personal friend who was the first British representative on the International Criminal Tribunal for the Former Yugoslavia. He later became the presiding judge in the Slobodan Milosevic trial, in which the former President of Serbia was being tried for war crimes, crimes against humanity, and genocide. Unfortunately, Judge May contracted a fatal illness during the trial before it was over and had to resign from the Tribunal. He died six months later, but not before he was knighted by Queen Elizabeth.

The first one week Sir Richard May Seminar held in September of 2005 was a great success. The 25 judges who participated in the seminar were ecstatic about the program, in which they learned about, what was for them, a whole new area of law and courts. The seminar included lectures by distinguished international jurists and site visits to the many places in The Hague that dealt with international law.

The Academy conducted six more such seminars and also a similar type of seminar on international human rights law in Strasbourg, France, the home of the European Court of Human Rights. The IJA planned for more seminars. Unfortunately, in 2008, the Academy had to terminate plans for future seminars beyond 2010, because the family supporting the New York foundation had all of its money invested with Bernard Madoff, the Wall Street swindler. They lost it all and the Academy lost $225,000 of grant money. This unfortunate experience demonstrated to me the perils of funding for international programs.

The Sir Richard May Seminar led to another satisfying experience. In 2010, in searching for new ideas for programs, I conceived of a film on international law. I made inquiries at various institutions whether such a film existed and was referred to a videotape that had been prepared by a U.S. law school. After viewing it, I found it uninspiring, to say the least – a professor sitting in a chair facing the camera, reading and lecturing about international law.

I decided to use the Sir Richard May Seminar as a background event for such a film. That same year, when we went to The Hague for the seminar, I took along a video camera and an intern from my office to film various parts of the seminar. I used my seminar lecture on the history of international law as the basis for the narrative of the film, and asked a former FJC colleague, a media technical expert, to help put together the narrative, the sequences, some appropriate photographs, and appropriate musical background.

I found this project to be exciting and stimulating. The end result was a 42-minute film titled '*Restoring Our Souls: A Film about War and Peace and International Law*'. The first part of the name for the film came from a phrase in a letter to me from a judge who had attended one of the Seminars. She wrote that the Seminar had 'restored her judicial soul'.

There was one other by-product of my work at the FJC and the IJA that has been a source of much satisfaction. This particular project was inspired by my experience as student editor-in-chief of the daily newspaper at the University of Virginia, the *Cavalier Daily*. While at the FJC, and with the approval of Judge Schwarzer, I developed an international judicial newspaper, titled the *International Judicial Observer,* which contained articles on the activities of the Center and those from other places and institutions about judicial and court activities, and court reform programs. With a very small staff (1), we were able to publish only four issues, mainly because of inadequate staffing. The effort, however, did lead to another publication, developed by me and friends from the American Society of International Law (ASIL).

In the winter of 2006, I made a trip to ASIL and met with several staff members about resurrecting the *International Judicial Observer.* We decided that a print version of the publication would not be possible, but that we could publish one online. The outcome of this and other meetings was the birth, in March, 2006, of an online judicial and court journal titled the *International Judicial Monitor.*

Published four times a year by the Academy, with circulation assistance from ASIL, it contains articles by judges and jurists on a variety of subjects relating to judges, courts, and international law. In 2011, the publishers LexisNexis selected the *International Judicial Monitor* as one of the 'top blogs' on the internet. In the spring of 2016, a celebration marked the 10th anniversary of the publication. During that time, we published 34 editions containing over 250 articles. The circulation of the *Monitor* now exceeds over 4,000 subscribers worldwide.

The current issue of the *International Judicial Monitor* can be viewed at judicialmonitor.org. Past issues can be accessed by clicking on 'Archives' at the top of the home page.

What has been my experience of working with international assistance programs for almost a quarter of a century? There have been several lessons that I have learned. The first is that legal and judicial reform is not something that can be accomplished overnight, or even within one or two years. It is a long, slow process which requires much persistence and perseverance. As one U.S. judge purportedly commented: "Judicial reform is not an activity to be engaged in by the faint-hearted."

When my tenure at the Federal Judicial Center started in the early 1990s, one of the practices of government organizations and private ones, at least in court reform efforts, was to send small delegations of knowledgeable persons to a particular country or region or city to participate in some conference or meeting or educational session to lecture for one or two days on the subject being considered for discussion and reform. I called these efforts 'parachute programs'.

They dropped people into an area for a short time for lectures or other educational sessions, who then departed. In my experience, sending 'experts' to another place for a short time to deliver a lecture or conduct a few learning sessions on law and courts and judges is, in most instances, a waste of time and money. Such programs are unlikely to motivate members of the audience to seek needed changes to existing institutions or practices. In planning for judicial and court reform, an effort must be made to take those judicial and court officers who are being targeted as reformists out of their home regions for considerable periods of time, such as one week or ten days or two weeks, to avoid distractions and allow for concentration on the learning sessions. The effort must be sustained over a period of weeks or months or even years, for any program to have a significant effect.

Another lesson that I have learned from my experiences at the FJC and the IJA is that very successful programs may fail the test of time. As even a casual observer to the current international scene can discern, political changes in any one country can occur rapidly and result in the country's abandonment of established institutions or reforms. This has happened in legal reform efforts in which I have been involved in Russia, one country in South America, and two countries in North Africa.

Yet another lesson I have learned is that neither the United States nor any other country can impose judicial and legal reforms from the outside. There must be committed persons within an individual country who have a passion for proposed reforms and are willing to take leadership roles in those reform efforts.

I can think of one particular program in which I was involved, in Romania, that was very successful and provides some confirmation for the above assertion. While at the Federal Judicial Center, I came into contact with a Romanian judge who eventually became the Romanian Minister of Justice. He had been impressed with the programs of the FJC and wanted to expose new magistrates in his country to the Center's programs, in anticipation of the development of a similar institution in Romania.

The Minister, eventually, was able to obtain a grant to the IJA from the U.S. Embassy in Bucharest, to bring one hundred new Romanian magistrate judges to Washington for a series of seminars on judicial reform issues. At the end of that program, with some leftover funds, the Romanian Ministry of Justice sent a six-member delegation to the International Judicial Academy for a two-week seminar on mediation. In the delegation was a court administrator from one of the smaller cities in Romania, the city of Craiova in the southwest part of the country. He was particularly enthusiastic about mediation and its possibilities for his country. He absorbed quickly the lessons the IJA presented about the establishment of a mediation program in a court system and methods for the conduct of mediation sessions.

I provided some advice about going forward with a program in his home city to establish a mediation service in the local court system. I had learned a particular lesson about court reform. That lesson was that a reform effort must be a measured effort, and that promoting reform that included too much, or was designed to move too fast, or was too complicated, was doomed to failure. I developed a simple slogan: "Start slow, start small, and start simple."

Using that as a formula, the Romanian court administrator went back to his home city and started to work.

The IJA recruited some of the members of the faculty, who had participated in the Washington seminar to go to Romania and conduct workshops for judges and court officers in Craiova, who would be involved in a start-up, court-annexed program. The Craiova group ultimately petitioned the Romanian parliament for a law permitting a mediation program in trial courts in the country. Armed with that legislation, the group established a mediation program for the local courts. When it proved successful, the enthusiastic court officer with whom I worked went around the country promoting mediation programs in local courts. The ultimate result of this effort was the eventual establishment of a mediation program in all of the courts in Romania. The success of this effort was due mostly to the enthusiastic young court administrator from Craiova.

When I was at the Federal Judicial Center, I developed some general principles for the conduct of international programs that have proved their worth during my time working in international development. First, I made the objective of the programs, the establishment of a legal system and court system in the particular country, embodying the characteristics mentioned earlier, one that is modern, fair, efficient, transparent, independent, and accessible. Such would be the mission of the IJA and the ultimate goal of each program. The different parts of each program would be designed and delivered with that end in mind. The general principles that I developed to achieve that goal were as follows:

1. Treat all program participants as honored guests. I did not want the Judicial Center or the IJA to take on an aura of an 'education factory', where we would just run the participants through a standardized program and be indifferent to them as individuals looking for enlightenment. So, we tried to make each participant feel welcome in our programs.
2. Develop specialized programs in accordance with the needs of the particular group or country.
3. Although many of the presentations in each program are usually lectures, advise the participants that questions and comments during the presentations would be welcome to stimulate discussion.
4. Limit the time of individual sessions. Humans are vulnerable to what I term 'information overload'. I have found that sessions that last one hour and fifteen

minutes before a break are the most effective, and do not result in inattention, exhaustion, or boredom.

5.   Conduct an introductory session at the beginning of the seminar or program. Provide a welcome message, review in detail the agenda with the delegation and offer opportunities for questions. Such action insures that all members of a delegation are on the same page during the conduct of the program.

6.   To the fullest extent possible, run the programs on time, from beginning to end. I was always aware that even the best planned and presented programs can turn sour if participants have to wait, whether it be for speakers, for a session to end, for a lunch break, or for adjournment time. We would always advise program participants that we would begin sessions each day on time and we would finish on time. That advice seemed to be very much appreciated.

7.   Include site visits in the program, interspersed among the lectures. Such an agenda provides an alternative way of imparting information and improving adult learning. Research has shown that adults learn better by experiencing a subject, rather than just hearing about it. A program that includes lectures reinforced by site visits provides more impact for the learning experience.

8.   Do not try to sell the U.S. legal system to the listeners. In the first place, such effort is offensive; it bespeaks too much of arrogance and patronizing. In addition, many of the U.S. methods in the conduct of its legal and court system would not work in other countries, given the way the U.S. legal system has developed over 400 years. I always advise the Academy's foreign visitors that although presentations might be based on experiences in the U.S., the participants should view the effort as one of offering a 'cafeteria of ideas' from which they could select methods or activities for use in their own countries.

9.   Stay with them – At the FJC and the IJA, I always made it a practice that I or one of my colleagues would be with the group at all times. This action provides a

zone of comfort for the participants, knowing that some local person is always around and ready to help if a problem or emergency arises. I remember one time the IJA hosted a group of judges/journalists representing the *China Court Daily*, a publication for judges and court officers throughout China. I arranged for all of their visits to journalism related organizations in the Washington area and then accompanied them on each site visit. They were so appreciative of my actions that when I visited Beijing the next year, which included a visit to the offices of the newspaper, they presented me with a book with photographs of their Washington visit and laudatory inscriptions (one inscription noted that 'We love you').

10. Limit the length of the program. When the Federal Judicial Center and the U.S. State Department first began conducting educational programs for judges from the new independent states of the former Soviet Union, we planned a three-week seminar. It was too long, and by the end of the second week, many of the participants were obviously tired and inattentive. The third week had much less impact than the first two. A two-week program is probably the outside limit for these kinds of programs; a one week or eight-day program seems to be the ideal.

11. Program quality trumps costs. The quality of the program takes precedence over efforts to 'cut corners', when considering expenses for developing the agenda for a seminar or other program and conducting it.

What has been the result of my activities at the FJC and the IJA, a period covering 25 years, and their impact on me personally? First, these activities rescued me from the malaise that was affecting me in law practice. Working for the federal government was, for me, and contrary to popular belief, stimulating and exciting. Having the opportunity to represent my country in overseas visits, which took me to almost all parts of the world, was a source of pride and accomplishment.

Second, they allowed me to become acquainted with many people involved in rule of law activities around the world, and to talk with them not only about the substance of educational programs and about international relations generally, but also about what was happening specifically in their countries and regions of the world. Most of the persons I met were interesting and dedicated and gave me a feeling of camaraderie in work that is noble. If I had to select one word that would describe my overall reaction to my experience in international relations, it would be 'enlightenment'. And that was a source of much satisfaction.

Another result of all of these activities has been a greater understanding of how the world operates, and how nations and individuals in other parts of the world function. It made me skeptical of ideologies and an admirer of practices that work in a particular country or region. The 'cafeteria of ideas' approach, mentioned earlier, provided reasons for program participants to be attentive to the different sessions making up the agenda.

Finally, I grew appreciative of the idea that the United States does not have all of the answers to the world's problems and cannot impose solutions on other countries without war, at least in the areas of courts and judges. It can, however, provide great insights into the principles and ideas that form the foundations of democracy, and provide valuable assistance for those countries that can be classified as developing democracies. That I have been a part of this effort and engaged with so many program participants in their efforts to make their countries better, has provided for me much pride and gratification.

That order, in the last year and a half, has not only been challenged but is being torn apart by the actions of the current president of the U.S. and his administration. The U.S., under his 'leadership' has abandoned carefully negotiated multi-lateral treaties in the areas of international trade, international security and climate change. Longtime allies of the United States which had also promoted a strong international order are also being abandoned.

It is a very discouraging situation for someone like me who has devoted a good part of his lift to the cause of international law and its ascendancy. However, my discouragement has been tempered by the remarks of Professor David A. Koplow Georgetown University Law Center in an article published in the *International Judicial Monitor* (IJM) titled '*The Fog of War: Is the Rule of Law Relevant?*' (*International Judicial Monitor*, Fall 2014 issue – available through the 'Archives' section of the current edition of the IJM, on the Home page at the top.)

Professor Koplow makes four observations which provide both hope and a beacon for future action, as follows:

1. International law does matter and will continue to do so.
2. Law is typically a lagging, not a leading, indicator of the human experience.
3. The United States is at its strongest and is most effective when it lives up to the rhetoric in support of the rule of law.
4. Traditional international law – in particular the law of armed conflict – provides an adequate basis for starting to address the new challenges.

Professor Koplow in his essay expands on each of these observations, all of which are well worth reading.

So the fight for the restoration of international law as the guiding mechanism for an international order most go on. I intend to be a part of that effort.

Dr. Apple talks with representatives of the Supreme People's Court of the People's Republic of China during a visit to Beijing in 2010.

Members of a Chinese judges delegation meet with representatives of the World Bank during a seminar in Washington conducted by the International Judicial Academy.

Dr. Apple addresses a judges' delegation at the Administrative
Office of the United States Courts in Washington, D.C.

Chapter 3
Short Stories
Judge Bogdan Jędrys
Cracow Regional Court, Poland

I

It was around 10 years ago. That day, I arrived home early about 3 pm. It was Friday, a really hot autumn day. I was tired after exhausting hearings in court. I got out of the car, I opened the garage and for a moment I was looking at flowers blooming in my garden which were still beautiful but already marked with the signs of autumn. Suddenly, my telephone rang. It was my colleague. "Bogdan, on Monday you are going to have a meeting with English judges on the EAW (European Arrest Warrant)!" The EAW is an arrest warrant valid throughout all member states of the European Union. Once issued, it requires another member state to arrest and transfer a criminal suspect or sentenced person to the issuing state, so that the person can be put on trial or complete a detention period.

I said, "OK, why not!"

On Monday, we were transferred from Heathrow Airport to one of the hotels in the Strand, Central London. I was accompanied by two other Polish judges, of which one was a president of one of the appellate courts in Northern Poland and an officer of the Polish Ministry of Justice.

The next day, we started meetings.

We visited the London court which deals with EAW cases and observed these cases. People who questioned the EAW were mainly Polish and Romanian citizens. They were arrested in England as a consequence of the EAW by authorities of their native countries. The Polish case was very typical. A defendant had been sentenced by a Polish court to a 2-year suspended sentence, together with a fine and damages for multiple offences of pickpocketing. Having been sentenced, he didn't fulfil the obligations imposed by the Polish court and he fled to England to avoid the sentence.

The Polish court imposed the suspended sentence and issued the EAW. He was arrested under the EAW in Great Britain, where he had been living and working for a couple of years. Before the hearing, he was advised confidentially by his girlfriend and a man who seemed to be a Polish-speaking, either a para-legal or a lawyer. They were speaking Polish, so despite a degree of confidentiality, I could understand them clearly.

During the case, his girlfriend was crying and screaming. He said to the judge that he was innocent. He explained that the Polish prosecutor had put a gun to his head to obtain a confession and said that this was often in Poland. Then, he continued that during hearings in the Polish court, he was hit heavily with a baton by the judge hearing the case. But he couldn't explain why he hadn't been arrested during the case in Poland and why he hadn't been sent to prison after such inhumane treatment. The decision of the first instance London court was appeal rejected, the EAW should be executed and the man extradited to Poland.

Then, we met English judges in the historical premises of the court. They explained us that they are overwhelmed with these types of cases and wished to find a way to decrease their number. Then they asked us about the particular issues connected with the aspects of Polish criminal law. I remember that it was a very interesting discussion, but the point which I never forgot were the differences between the practical effect of common and continental law. Certainly, during my studies I learnt about common law but then in London I could experience its operation in practice.

During the discussion, I tried to convince my English colleagues that we were bound by the rule of ex-officio prosecuting even in minor cases, and in this respect, we, as Polish judges, have no discretion.

I remember at some point, a charming judge, whilst drinking a nice cup of tea, told me that she could not believe that we as judges could not stop this situation. But I had to tell her that we could not and to some extent we still cannot. The discussion went on and both sides concluded that we had to put Polish lawmakers under pressure and as a consequence we confronted the representative of the Ministry. It was the only time when I was able to do so being backed by my English colleagues. The significance of this is that, as a judge, I feel constantly attacked by politicians.

That is the point from which I have begun to share my opinions with English judges and made friends with them, not only on a professional basis, but also on the basis of our common admiration of English gardens!

I have since given up EAW and extradition cases and currently I undertake mainly the most serious criminal cases. However, I believe that the ideas which we discussed with our English colleagues fostered and perpetuated ongoing cooperation. On the other hand, in the wake of the British decision to leave European Union, the discussion on EAW remains an open question.

It is time that I give some basic idea of my writing. I am not writing a regular narrative and do not pretend to give the account of the events in which I participated; or on the other hand, elaborate on legal issues; but only describe, in rather light form, the most relevant international experiences from the standpoint of a Polish, European judge.

II

"Bogdan, you must not go to Naples! It is Africa! They are Africans! You will probably die there …" the words of advice which I was given by one of the lawyers from Northern Italy. It was round 3 a.m. and we were about to finish the 60th Birthday Celebrations of an Italian judge based in one of the North Italian cities. It was buzzy celebration with live music and fireworks. It took place in a palace which our hosts were in course of restoring in the manner of the 1st French Empire.

It took me less than 9 hours to get form Northern Italy to Naples.

When I was approaching Naples, the comfortable motorway from Rome changed into wide cobbled streets. By the way, most of roads in Naples are like this. Later on, one of Naples prosecutors explained that it is intentionally kept like that to avoid speeding. I was going through the suburb of this colossal city when all of the sudden I was struck by the magnitude of Naples' harbor, which seemed to be the heart of the city. "Yes, it is," said aforementioned prosecutor. "It is … the biggest European hub for *contrabandisti*! We still try to fight it," he added after a moment.

While driving in the harborside area, my satellite navigation suddenly ceased to operate. I asked a passing man to give me directions but he said he didn't know where I wanted to go. After a couple of seconds, he ran towards my car and forcibly opened the door and sat down next to me. My first thought was, *That's the end of my life, he will kill me soon, the lawyer from Northern Italy was right* ... But to my surprise, he turned to be quite a nice guy, especially when I spoke with him in Italian, and using the sat nav in his smartphone, he led me to the right place!

My hotel in Naples was situated in the old part of the city, and every day I heard the matins church bells, a melodious tone which was killed by the hum and murmur of the city which surged with passing morning hours like oceanic waves. It was next to the harbor where the ferries were anchored. Later on, when my wife arrived, we took a wonderful trip by ferry to Ischia Isle, where *'La Mortella',* a beautiful garden of Sir William Walton, the renowned British composer, is situated.

My apartment in Naples was run by a worker from the Ukraine. He spoke Polish like many Ukrainians. "I hate this city. If I stay here any longer I will die," he said later on. Then he added, "Unfortunately, I have to stay here still for some time whilst I save money, as I am in the course of constructing a house for myself and my fiancée near Lvov, Ukraine …"

Naples courts are located in two skyscrapers in the *Centro Direzionale* district. It contains all Neapolitan courts and it is said to be even bigger than the court in Rome. "In course of construction, these buildings were set on fire. Investigation still has not revealed whether it was the developer or Gomorrah *soci* who had set fire," the Italian prosecutor explained.

They are both sealed buildings, but when you manage to enter, you feel like you are in the midst of an incredibly busy railway station. Judges, prosecutors, defendants, witnesses, experts, and lawyers were hurrying, shouting and smoking everywhere in a very nervous way. In the canteen, you can even have a wine or a shot of hard liquor.

All of a sudden, a speaker announced the commencement of the case in which Roberto Saviano was going to witness. Let me mention that Roberto Saviano is the famous Italian writer and reporter who, in his novel *Gomorrah*, revealed top secrets of that criminal organization.

Top security measures were in place, but we managed to enter the courtroom. The huge tension was felt. The courtroom was full of reporters who were reporting it live for Italian Television. Roberto Saviano was guarded by five police officers. He gave his testimony, and then he answered several questions asked by prosecutor, defendants, and defendants' lawyers, but the court did not ask any question.

All the defendants, including *gomoristi* and their lawyers, were provisionally arrested under the charge of threatening Saviano and participated in this court session via satellite transmission. I thought to myself, *Strange ... no questions asked by the court in such a high-profile case ... top security case and reporters were allowed to enter ... strange.* Then we visited different divisions of the Naples Court, and I saw judges everyday struggling with an incredibly large number of cases.

"You know, Bogdan ... several years ago, we introduced in criminal cases an inquisitorial system ... but it hasn't worked ... that's why the court remained silent in Saviano's case," the prosecutor said. Asked about the relationship with Northern Italy, he sighed and said, "Bogdan, you can't even imagine how diverse Italy is."

I hope this insight is of some interest and requires some comment. An adversarial system in criminal cases had been also introduced in Poland, but it lasted only 9 months when the government and MP's decided to reintroduce an inquisitorial system which was almost always in power in Poland. This controversial decision was taken as a consequence, in part due to the 'failure' of the Italian adversarial system.

For clarification, I must add that by inquisitorial_system, I mean a procedure in which the presiding judge is not a passive recipient of information, but rather he or she is primarily responsible for gathering of the evidence necessary to resolve the case.

Referring to our European history, I recognize its irony. Poland, as a homogenous country in the course of history, had been partitioned and lost its independence, and after regaining it, had to unify three legal systems, namely Prussian, Russian, and Austrian, which to some extent has threatened its stability. But in contrast, diversified Italy is bound by one system of law.

I still admire Italian judges for their constant struggle to apply common rules in their diversified society!

III

It was the time when I hosted two young Romanian judges in Cracow. I asked them how the high-profile case in which there were several judges provisionally arrested had finished. They answered that they had been all sentenced to deprivation of liberty which ranged from two to six years. "The judge who rendered this sentence is our emblem, a hero indeed!" they added.

Two years earlier, I had visited Romanian courts and law enforcement institutions. Among others, we visited a court in which there was an exhibition showing a history of the court which contained a torture chamber.

I noticed that the majority of the Romanian judicial staff was very young. They were predominantly women, 30 years old or younger. They were perfectly trained and they did their job with great commitment. They were very open to new ideas. They were deeply interested in the Italian system as they were about to implement an amendment of their criminal procedure to resemble the Italian one.

Every day we discussed different problems. For instance, how to handle multiple prosecutors' requests for provisional arrest if based on complex factual basis, especially in fraud cases within the 48-hour European time limit. In the course of this visit, a bombshell occurred on Romanian TV. Several Romanian judges dealing with real estate cases were charged with fraud and detained by Police forces.

The next day, they were convoyed to court. When the detainees were brought to the court, it was full of reporters and the case was transmitted live. We were allowed into the courtroom but then the presiding judge ordered secrecy and we were asked to leave. The decision was provisional arrest applied.

After some time, I saw one of those women judges in prison. She was in a single cell. She was reading a book and waiting for the outcome of the appellate measure she filed to the court of higher instance. The appeal was dismissed when the court ruled the provisional arrest was valid.

We discussed that case widely, although that main finding of the investigation was secret. My colleague judges and prosecutors from Italy and Germany could not find any similar case in the modern history of our countries. Our Romanian host were shocked too and tried to avoid this subject. But we all felt that this was a premonition of something wrong for the future, and we were right, because the present-day international terrorism situation in Russia or in Turkey threatens judges' impartiality, especially as executive authorities tend to have more and more unsupervised power in relation to human liberties.

IV

"What's going on here? Are we in court or in a museum? We have been visiting this court every day for a week and no defendants, witnesses, or lawyers can be seen! It is incredible!" exclaimed my Italian colleague, judge d'instruction in Palermo, Sicily. "What a difference to our courts!" Spanish and French colleagues added.

They were right because we had been visiting the historical premises of one of the courts in Northern Germany and could see only judges and clerks working quietly in their chambers. It was unlike English, Spanish, French, Romanian, or Italian courts which I visited throughout the years.

In the end, when we could observe court hearings, what I saw was a very relaxed procedure both in civil and criminal cases. A judge simply discussed with the parties, legal and factual issues and then pronounced a judgement which was, in civil and family cases, recorded on a voice recorder with the agreement of all parties. I remember the irritation of one young German judges when a witness openly lied to him supporting a defendant. My Italian colleague said, "Why is he irritated? In Italy witnesses usually lie! And I saw an evil grin on his face."

"In Poland, as well," I confirmed, and I am sure that my face expression was the same.

We discussed this difference later on and our German colleagues explained to us that they act in full accordance with parties' counsels, which was then confirmed during our meetings with members of the bar and prosecutors. I still cannot understand how it worked but it really did.

We then visited several law enforcement agencies as well as social care or municipal. Everywhere, I could notice perfect German organization. They tackled immigration problems, sensibly providing for almost all immigrant families, who were expected to be admitted to stay in Germany, separate abodes.

V

Generally, but not exclusively, my international experiences are based on my participation in 'Exchange Programme' by European Judicial Training Network.

Writing these words, I am also ahead of another big experience, as I was 10 years ago, which is the conference of British judges in Cracow in September 2016, which 70 British judges will be attending.

These short stories are mainly illustration to the questions which have been bothering me for years. I mean, what is the relationship between law enforcement and independence of countries? To what degree are my decisions determined by my social or national environment? What is the psychological significance of judges' age? Should a judge follow patterns of renowned judges or always find his or her own conclusions? What are particular social or professional qualities which make judges' decisions sensible? What should the organization of judges' work look like, especially to be efficient? Which procedure is better to tackle serious, mainly terroristic crimes or to maintain standards, should it be adversarial or inquisitorial?

I haven't got all the right answers for these questions and many others which could be asked, but I am sure that each international experience deepens my knowledge of those problems and finally enforces my work as a judge.

OBSERVATORY JUDGES SEMINAR
Alicante 7th - 8th November 2016

Judge Jedrys with a group of international judges.

Chapter 4
Judges and the Rule of Law
Chief Judge John R. Tunheim
United States District Court – Minnesota

The mountain streams are fighting their own losing battle in this Kosovar spring. The rivers' valiant attempt to wash away the blood, the tears and the anger that blanket this ancient Balkan land are having little effect. As spring comes early to Kosovo this year, there is dashed hope and fewer expectations. What little patience remains is faltering and the warmth of the springtime sun brings no joy; it can only predict hotter days to come. Time has become the latest enemy in Kosovo.

I wrote that passage in my journal while riding in a very uncomfortable armored vehicle between the devastated Kosovo cities of Pristina and Prizren in the early spring of 2000. A journey that today takes less than an hour was then a nearly four-hour drive on battered roads. I was there at the request of the U.S. State Department to help the United Nations determine how to return the war-torn province to the rule of law and at the time, how to jump start a legal system in serious disarray or missing entirely. I was expressing my frustration at the slow pace of change, at the difficulty to starting a legal system in a region where a different system had existed before the war. Potential independence was exciting for the people I met, but there was no real concept of the state and no real understanding of the common good in a clannish culture.

Most of the people had lived in a parallel society for many years with shadow courts and substandard education. The revenge instinct was just beneath the surface. To make matters worse, the post-war conditions at the time were primitive – electricity was rare, running water was sporadic, the air was thick with harsh coal smoke, hotels were missing windows, and travel was difficult. Life today in Kosovo has improved very much, thanks in no small way to the return of the rule of law.

Why is development of the rule of law important, especially when a territory is faced with enormous challenges? After all, we cannot and should not force a people to develop democratic institutions and the rule of law. Forcing people to accept democracy without understanding why and how is a sure prescription for failure. We have seen many examples over the years. And we know democracy is not a perfect institution. Most people in the world do not understand the universal values underlying government by the people and how to apply these values successfully.

Judicial independence means something different depending on where you are. Even judges who strongly desire independence in their work, simply may not know what to do or how to change their system. Developing the rule of law takes a long time and can be very messy.

The answer, to me, is clear: democracy and the rule of law present the best opportunity to provide the most people with the most benefits of a just society. The rule of law is the foundation for justice, for economic development, for human rights, and for social order. Developing the rule of law involves teaching people to think differently about their world. But for those involved in this important work, we must constantly remind ourselves that this is not a cookie cutter world – the rule of law can be different in different places.

First, it is vitally important to understand the history of a people and the culture of a place. Without such understanding, change cannot take place. And second, we always need to base our work on universal truths and values about justice and human rights. International covenants, the agreements reached by most of the countries of the world, are the place to begin any discussion of the rule of law. We practice the rule of law quite well in America although we have our flaws, some very serious. There is an intense curiosity in the world about the American system.

I will answer any question about our system, but I will never urge our system on another country. The rule of law must fit within the history and culture and understandings of people who do not have our background but share our desire for justice and human rights.

Today presents a dangerous and uncertain time, a time when terrorist attacks on civilians are commonplace and wars break out without warning. Regions once obscure, suddenly burst violently into public view and face a long and treacherous road to rehabilitation and healing. Increasingly, western democracies have taken responsibility for the reconstruction. Small, struggling 'new' countries stagger as they make the difficult transition from totalitarian societies into countries trying to respect democratic values.

Today, it is even more essential to focus the attention of the world on the best hope for a safe and secure future: the rule of law. And in my view, judges can and should play a role in helping develop, nurture, and sustain the rule of law.

Myriad professionals are engaged in the international marketplace of programs on rule of law – contractors, international groups, governments, non-governmental organizations, and many more. Some programs have achieved a level of effectiveness, but much money could be better spent. The best programs, I have observed, are small and personal. They focus patiently on building a strong foundation, one block at a time, for the rule of law. They are programs like the terrific American Bar Association's Rule of Law Initiative, with which I have been involved, a program that has sent highly qualified staff and committed volunteers throughout Central and Eastern Europe, and Eurasia since the fall of the Soviet Union, and now, throughout the world.

The best programs focus on all aspects of the justice system, but they recognize one key factor – the important role of judges. Judges are on center stage throughout the world – critical to building a lasting rule of law. And who can best teach, encourage, and convince judges to be independent and fair? Judges – democratic judges with their extraordinary experience as independent judges in systems governed by the rule of law.

For nearly as long as I have been a federal district court judge, I have been a willing volunteer – willing to go to the Balkans to help build new judiciaries and willing to go to the old former Soviet republics to help teach and nurture judges on how to be independent, ethical, and fair. There have been times when I have questioned my willingness – Siberia in the winter is no one's idea of comfort, nor is staying in dilapidated hotels in the early years of Kosovo independence, without reliable heat, water, or electricity. Nights in small hotels in the rural cities of Central Asia surely lack the comforts of almost anywhere else in the world. But the inconveniences have always been worth it.

I have always learned much more than I have been able to give to the many judge colleagues I have met throughout the world. I have helped them, but in return, their questions and observations and insights have made me a better judge.

My international experience over the years has become too extensive to catalog. I have worked on criminal justice reform in Russia and many of the former republics of the Soviet Union. My work in Kosovo has included many dozens of trips, first helping the United Nations establish a functioning legal system and helping to nurture that system, then playing a central role in the drafting of Kosovo's Constitution, and now working closely with the fledgling constitutional court. The work in Uzbekistan on human rights and legal reform is starting to bear fruit. Lately, I have been working on helping judges learn how to better handle terrorism cases, in the Balkans, the Middle East, Africa, and South Asia. From jury trials in Georgia, to criminal procedure reform in the Ukraine, to election reform in Bangladesh, and to codes of ethics in Uzbekistan, I have truly enjoyed the many individual conversations I have had with judges – judges who, like me, desire both independence and allegiance to the rule of law.

Much of my international work has involved me in two very different types of situations: the post-crisis, immediate challenges facing the legal system in a devastated environment like Kosovo, and the more long-range rule of law development issues typical of countries still emerging slowly from a past in which the rule of law was recognized in name only. The long-term challenge – to build a fair and independent justice system – is the same, but the immediate challenges are strikingly different.

Post-Crisis Challenges

Bosnia-Herzegovina, East Timor, Kosovo, Afghanistan, Iraq, South Sudan, and so many more countries have faced and continue to address enormous post-crisis challenges. Increasingly, regions which emerge from a violent conflict have legal systems with an almost inconceivable range of immediate needs, the most important of which is to move quickly to get a basic legal system in place and functioning.

When I first visited Kosovo in January 2000, nine months after the end of the NATO campaign, judges and prosecutors were appointed, but they were sitting in empty, cold, and damaged courthouses with no real ability to do their critical work. Crime and interethnic violence were epidemic and opportunistic, embracing the empty vacuum in the criminal justice system. Peacekeepers helped, but they have different interests than a legal system. In this type of environment, without a functioning legal system, the security situation deteriorates quickly.

The immediate issues in Kosovo were, I am sure, similar to the issues in other post-crisis situations. For starters, what should be the applicable law? A crippling uncertainty cost valuable time in Kosovo. Yugoslav law had been applied discriminatorily and the judges refused to use it. When the United Nations finally determined, after a long false start, that the law from a decade earlier would be applied, the judges were enthusiastic, but just what was the law in 1989 – in a simpler, bygone Communist controlled era? There were few up-to-date codebooks. The necessary development of new criminal and civil laws, and procedure codes take time – too much time for a system in crisis.

As in any crisis, one must keep in mind that the perfect is the enemy of the good. I tried to convince the judges to simply use common sense – and apply a blend of the laws they knew. The details would come later, but the crisis was urgent.

Where were the lawyers who can represent criminal defendants? Training for judges, lawyers, and new lawyers was urgent. Judges had experience as judges, but no experience at independent thinking. How do you instill confidence and control in judges accustomed to waiting for instructions? How about security for courthouses and judges? Threats were commonplace, how can you expect fair decisions without some level of security?

Courthouses lacked electricity – so they lacked computers, metal detectors, telephones, and safes – all essential to a court system. Libraries and files were gone, destroyed or taken. New police needed to be trained and there was little effective communication between the temporary international police and the prosecutors with whom they need to work. Rival political parties were 'appointing' their own rival courts and proclaiming sovereignty – how do we get control and push the rule of law into the vacuum?

Temporary detention facilities needed to be established and prisons rebuilt. Many accused criminals were being simply released, and others were being held without hearings or judicial review for long periods of time. Who could deliver the summons for the judges? Who could escort prisoners to court? While I was first in Kosovo, one judge had established the practice of driving an accused criminal back to a detention center after a hearing – there was no other way, he said. And at the time, he was absolutely right.

In Kosovo, as in all of the recent post-crisis regions, the most serious threat was the danger of ethnic violence, which threatens any progress a legal system can make. In Kosovo, it was an important goal to create a multi-ethnic judiciary, a goal that still presents challenges seventeen years later. Generations of bitter conflict and rivalry are not forgotten overnight, but the success of any post-crisis government depends on its ability to work at including all ethnic groups. Because of ethnic rivalries, the temporary solution of appointing international judges to hear significant cases is still being used in Kosovo.

In time, but surely not overnight, a well-functioning legal system was established in Kosovo. A judicial council ensures strong appointments of judges, a modern criminal code and criminal procedure code are well understood, security is better and the government is stable. Ethnic rivalries still threaten democratic values, but democracy has taken hold.

Fundamental to a long-term stable democracy is, of course, a well-written constitution, a constitution that provides the basic guarantees of human rights and establishes a government structure that will enhance and protect the rule of law. Although it surely can be argued today that the most basic foundational documents in a new democracy are the international covenants that protect human rights, a constitution is essential to enshrine the rule of law.

After seven years of relative stability under the United Nations administration and the continuing failure of negotiations with Serbia, it was time to push for independence. Led by the United States and the European missions in Kosovo, we developed an international and local team to draft a constitution that would be ready for Independence Day. Much of the work was funded by USAID which maintains a significant investment in the development of the rule of law.

An assessment was essential. What problems needed to be addressed in the Constitution and what goals were important to Kosovo? What regional and cultural aspects of Kosovo society needed to be fully respected? What process would facilitate not only the drafting of a document, but also reaching the difficult decisions that needed to be made in order to achieve consensus? Who would be the higher-level political leadership team that can make decisions that commission members could not? Who has the requisite legal and drafting skills together with sensitivity to all the people of Kosovo? Who could represent the interests of the various ethnic groups and also have the knowledge, skills, and experience necessary to do a difficult job?

In addition, what foundational documents were essential to consult in the development process? International covenants, prior constitutions in Yugoslavia and its republics, new constitutions in the Balkan territories and other recent constitutional drafting all needed to be reviewed. What type of training program would be necessary to ensure that all options were considered and fully understood? All commission members needed to be equally conversant in this process and understand both the possibilities and the limitations of their work. How could we design a decision-making process that would achieve consensus relatively quickly and eliminate serious and time-consuming roadblocks? How could we achieve some level of public input in the process, a task made extremely difficult because Kosovo was not yet a country and the United Nations resolution intended to guide this process had not yet been adopted because of opposition from Serbia. And finally, how could we document the process and the decisions made so that Kosovo would have some written history of how the Constitution was developed.

At the outset of the constitutional development process in March 2007, Kosovo had a number of very important goals. First, to draft a document that would be broadly acceptable to the people of Kosovo, a document that not only 'belonged' to Kosovo but was also acceptable and impressive to the rest of the world. Second, it was important to provide a constitution that would help ensure broad international acceptance of the new country and quick recognition of Kosovo independence. And, third, Kosovo still hopes for eventual admission and membership into the European Union. It was thought that making the best decisions for the constitution could help speed that important process.

In addition, the new constitution could not ignore the history of ethnic violence and the widespread belief that non-majority populations would not receive a fair shake or even protection from the new government. We also tried to respect Kosovo's promises throughout the failed mediation process with Serbia. Protections for non-majority populations were an important guarantee.

The process that began in March 2007 was involved, lengthy, and difficult at times. Involving representatives of the non-majority communities was especially challenging. The consistent pressure applied by the American Ambassador, who ensured the funding of the process, was critical. When Kosovo declared its independence in February 2008, the draft constitution was published immediately, and after several months of public input, was presented to the government in April and ratified in June. It has functioned well in the nearly decade-old democracy. While it surely was not critical for judges to be involved in the process, a judge's experience with interpreting constitutions and anticipating the many issues that will arise in interpretation was very helpful. In addition, a judge's perspective on the development of the legal system's principles is critical.

The crisis in Kosovo gives some clues to the challenges faced in Afghanistan, Iraq, and other countries still ravaged by war. It is important simply to jump-start the legal system, to get judges working at resolving disputes and ensuring some brand of justice before the situation deteriorates further. When judges claim they have no code to apply, you simply have to help them use common sense. Most of the time that is what judges do. Judges cannot wait for direction. Problems can be corrected later. The immediate results may not be perfect, and indeed, may not even be pretty. But there is time to work on long-range solutions, to start putting in place the foundation for the rule of law. Getting started is the key. Detailed criminal procedure codes, judicial councils, and constitutions will come later.

Long Range Development

Most of the rule of law work I have done as a judge involves the effort to improve the legal systems of the countries of Eastern Europe, Eurasia, South Asia, and the Middle East, where the history or tradition of the rule of law is spotty. This is slow and patient work that requires a long view toward the future. Much of the ongoing work in Kosovo, now years after the crisis, has moved into longer range future development.

I have found that the best, most effective work is done after taking the time to observe a country's system, to listen to its judges and participants and to focus on the particular urgent needs. Every country and region is different and cookie cutter programs are not very effective. For example, Lithuania needed training in sophisticated approaches to organized crime, while Uzbekistan needed training in basic human rights issues. The different needs of the two systems are stark. Despite sharing the Soviet legacy, the two countries now are at very different stages of development of the rule of law.

The most important ongoing work, in my view, is the effort to encourage and convince judges to be independent. The lack of judicial independence remains the most significant barrier to effective administration of a legal system. Many countries face structural impediments, particularly where judges can be removed for no reason at all, but in other countries, the basic constitutional framework is there and progress on the path to independence is up to the judges.

What works best? In my experience, nothing is better than judge-to-judge dialogue. Sharing ideas, discussing why certain procedures are followed, understanding the lives and histories of judges, demonstrating how to do basic tasks like developing a record, and just plain talking and telling stories of life on the bench. The time is valuable, and I learn so much from these discussions. Western judges – with a long practiced significant role in the legal system – command respect in other countries. I have found that the respect gets judges' attention and offers an opening – an opportunity to share ideas.

Unless the conversations are approached as equals sharing their experiences, the respect can quickly dissipate. We have many flaws in our western systems and it is very important to acknowledge them, but we also have so much experience to share. And our independence is what eastern European and Eurasian judges crave, despite their lack of experience in and understanding of true independence. Structural independence is important but teaching judges how to be independent thinkers is far more important. If you can convince a judge to discuss reasons why they feel they cannot be impartial or independent – that is a very successful conversation and an important step toward changing the legal environment.

Role-playing hearings and trials are also very useful. Foreign judges who have had the opportunity to visit the United States have seen our hearings, but most judges will never have that opportunity. Demonstrating, for example, how to conduct a change of plea hearing or a sentencing procedure can be very valuable for judges who desperately would like to develop more expedited criminal proceedings.

I have found that discussions about judicial independence which include prosecutors are less than productive. Throughout many regions of the world, judges will gain independence and authority primarily from prosecutors, and the rivalry can diminish any chances for an effective discussion.

Ethics issues – again in a discussion with a small group of judges – are also effective teaching tools. If hypotheticals are well-crafted, the discussion and differences of opinion can open the door to real discussion of substantive difficulties that judges face everywhere.

Human rights is the primary long-range concern of any evaluator of a legal system – and it is, of course, a primary concern of the United States in assessing foreign countries and encouraging the development of the rule of law. It really needs to be a focal point, carefully done, of any rule of law assistance program. In my experience, U.S. State Department reports and human rights criticisms have limited success in improving human rights. Judges throughout the world share human rights concerns; the primary problem is convincing judges that they have the authority and the power to do something about human rights violations.

Perhaps the best approach is to try to instill in the new generations of lawyers the courage to challenge human rights violations in court. New generations, after all, are much less inflicted with the old way of thinking. Human rights clinics in law schools can be very effective in generating the necessary skills and passion to raise the issues. Building effective bar associations, and particularly, criminal defense counsel associations also have potential.

But my focus is the judge. Will a judge act if he or she is aware that an accused has been coerced? That is a difficult question in some parts of the world. Many countries have in their laws or codes an equivalent to our exclusionary rule, but it is not often utilized. Again, a dialogue on human rights issues with judges, together with examples of the effectiveness of excluding evidence gathered improperly, is a start. It is an important long-range concern and our ability to convince judges to protect human rights, to use the laws that are available to them, is worth a substantial investment of time.

I also spend time encouraging judges to establish judges' associations. There is strength in numbers and judges working together can and should have an impact, not only on important judicial independence and human rights issues, but also on working conditions and livable salaries.

Judges in many of the countries of the world have a long distance to travel on the road to independence. Some judges are further down the road than others. The judges do not often command much respect, in large part because judges were tools of governments in non-democratic times, and people know nothing different today. That is why the experiences of American and western European judges – independent judges in systems governed by the rule of law – can be so valuable to judges in other regions. A discussion of how we got to where we are today is of great value to them. All it takes is one idea to grow. All countries have faced difficult rule of law challenges – how we learn from these challenges to make our legal systems better is the key.

It is still a time of transition for so many of the new countries. Whether they develop into functioning democracies supported by the rule of law is still an open question. The judges in these countries have an opportunity to play a significant role in developing the rule of law. The experiences of western judges, as independent judges in a system grounded in the rule of law, can be invaluable to these judges who are trying to take the first small steps to independence.

I have seen much progress in many of the countries in which I have worked with judges. In other countries, I sometimes feel like we take one step forward and two steps back. Patience and dedication are essential, and in the end, very much worth the time and effort. Building the rule of law to provide justice for everyone takes much time.

Whether I am working in the chaos of a post-crisis region or I am working in the relative calm of a quiet emerging democracy, I like to think back to the image of the unrelenting mountain streams I saw on my first visit to Kosovo. The rivers were working so hard to wash away a terrible past. Although success was modest then, the mountain streams are a constant energy.

Today they are having much more success than in that warm early spring of 2000. I like to think that the rule of law has had a lot to do with the positive changes in that ancient Balkan land and in so many other places in the world. I am convinced, development of the rule of law is the best hope for a world that remains dangerous and uncertain, a world waiting for the mountain streams to bring justice and peace.

Chapter 5
The Challenge of International Judicial and Court System Reform
Dr. Markus Zimmer

Good Morning, Sofia

I awoke with a start and sat bolt upright in the low, narrow bed; eyes shifting about, desperate for something to focus on in the darkness. The intense heat in the room had scorched the air. Blinking hurt and my skull throbbed. The threadbare sheets were patched with sweat. I reached to switch on the flimsy lamp next to the bed, yelping as my fingers took a jolt from the faulty connection. I looked at my watch; 1:48 a.m., 26 January 1992.

Seven hours earlier, I had been on Lufthansa flight 325 from Frankfurt, having accepted a very young ABA-CEELI's invitation for a two-week leave of absence, to travel to post-revolution Bulgaria to work with its courts. It seemed like a noble endeavor, exporting American superiority in the technocracy of court management. The plane touched down on the dimly illuminated tarmac. A ground crew wheeled a rusting Balkan Air staircase up to the jet. Once down the stairs, I climbed into a creaking old bus with rust holes in the floor revealing the tarmac. The bus lumbered over to the 1940s-vintage terminal where I joined a mad rush to long lines for passport and visa control. Dour agents, clothed in drab Soviet military garb, glared from behind smudged tinted glass and examined our papers.

Bill Meyer, CEELI's first liaison, snaked a tiny car through Sofia's dreary streets, barely illuminated by rationed electricity, to a Communist apparatchik hotel. I checked in, reluctantly surrendering my passport. A diminutive elevator squealed painfully as it lurched upward, opening on an unventilated hallway with worn, stained carpeting curled up on either side. I found my room, opened the window to cool it down. Dead tired, I switched off the light, but sleep was elusive. I'd awake chilled and shaking because I'd opened the window too far. I'd adjust it, go back to sleep, and wake up 40 minutes later, because the heat from the radiator, with the control knob rusted wide open, had built up. At 5:45 a.m., I jumped as a piercing screech filled the room. I opened my eyes to the first light of a smoggy grey dawn, climbed up from the bed, and peered out the window. Down on the plaza, an antiquated tram lumbered along, metal wheels squealing against steel rails. It was painted yellow with CAMEL in large blue letters. Ten minutes later, another screeched by, this one bright red and white with MARLBORO in large black letters. My welcome to Bulgaria began with an introduction to the business interests of American tobacco, the baggage of capitalist democracy.

We spent the next two weeks visiting courts of various jurisdictions and size in Sofia, Smolyan, and Plovdiv. The days were long as I undertook, through interpreters, to fathom how the system functioned. The first-time early 1990s U.S. visitor was taken aback by conditions in Eastern Europe's post-Soviet courts. Some public intake offices featured, as décor, posters of semi-nude women. Equipment typically ranged from 50s-vintage typewriters to primitive desktops. Filings were sewn by hand or secured by string into flimsy case file folders stacked on sagging shelves or on floors where scavenging rats gnawed them. Case information was compiled by hand in thick registers. Lower-level judges were crowded by groups into small offices with barely sufficient space to accommodate a visiting litigant or court clerk. Under the hybrid socialist/civil law systems of post-Soviet bloc states, chief judges doubled as chief administrative officers, their chambers often serving as congestion points in the court business pipeline.

One morning, we interviewed a Supreme Court justice, a cordial jurist with decades of experience. His office dimensions were 12' x 12'. Two weathered desks butted up against each other, stacked high with case files. On each was an old 50s-vintage typewriter with a stack of used carbon paper. Bulgarian justices shared tiny offices and were entitled neither to secretaries nor law clerks, a stark contrast to how our SCOTUS justices are liberally staffed in luxuriously appointed, spacious suites, and independently determine their workload.

We ranged over topics including decades of Communist rule and suppression of the judiciary. As a host, the justice was honest, friendly, humorous, and as curious about us as we were about him. At the end of the interview, he produced a bottle of rakia, Bulgaria's national drink, a plum brandy that, to the uninitiated, tastes like a mixture of low-octane gasoline, jalapeno extract, and corn syrup. He scrounged up cups of varied shape, size, and sanitation, poured us a healthy belt, then toasted democracy. Seven months earlier, post-revolution Bulgaria had conducted its first democratic elections since 1931, electing dissident Zhelyu Zhelev, its first non-communist head of state.

Given government inertia, most civil service positions remained occupied by Communists who viewed us with suspicion, contempt and curiosity. Persuading them to embrace reform in court governance, management, and administration would be a function of building trust and friendship, of downplaying the rancorous political divisiveness spawned during the ruinous Cold War. Invoking ideology inevitably resulted in counter-productive diversions that squandered valuable time.

* * * * * * * *

A Swiss émigré, who became a naturalized U.S. citizen in my teens, I have had the privilege of advancing the rule of law my entire professional career. It began at Washington DC's Federal Judicial Center, where I developed curricula and facilitated training throughout the U.S. for federal trial and magistrate judges, public defenders, court managers and administrators, and probation and pretrial services officers, among others. After 10 years, I moved back to the west to manage and administer Utah's busy federal trial court. Five years into my tenure, I began to volunteer as a court and judicial systems advisor in the emerging democracies of Central and Eastern Europe. By 2016, I had worked on the ground with the leadership of 30 judiciaries in all populated regions of the globe. Bulgaria was my first assignment.

Are Those Bullet Holes in the Walls Above My Bed?

On a crisp fall morning, shafts of brilliant sunlight streamed through the French doors that led out to a balcony overlooking the main town square as I awoke. It was 1994 in Osijek in eastern Croatia. My assignment was to deliver a lecture for regional judges and court staff in Osijek's main courthouse, a few miles to the west of where the Balkan War with Serbia raged. The previous evening's discussion over a late dinner of meat, cheese, peasant bread, and slivovitz, Croatia's rakia, with Dean Lauc of the J.J. Strossmayer University Law Faculty had included my hotel. The room he'd reserved for me had been used by every ilk of politician, from Nazi to Communist, to bark from its balcony at sullen crowds in the square.

Lying on my back, I focused on a hole in the wall, about five feet up from my bed, the size of a silver dollar with shredded edges angled inward. My gaze came on another, then another, and yet another, all curiously similar. It slowly dawned on me that these were bullet holes. Following my lecture, several local judges invited me to lunch at a nearby restaurant. The group got a bit carried away with a series of slivovitz toasts to Bulgarian/American friendship. I reciprocated. Add to that a several-course meal of lamb, fowl, potatoes, and sundry other sides and garnishes, and a rather groggy group of us filed out two hours later.

On a silly whim, I asked the presiding judge whether we could drive to the war zone whose boundaries were patrolled by U.N. troops. A compliant host, he ushered me into a small court car, placed a blinking blue emergency light on the roof, and drove off. Half an hour later, non-military traffic had disappeared. Ten minutes later, barriers appeared that required us to execute zigzags. Posted every 50 yards were multi-lingual signs warning of warzone danger. Then the road was blocked by a thick, chest-high cement barrier. The judge pulled off the road near a small guard station next to an armored U.N. troop carrier. As we exited, an intimidating muscular and grimacing soldier approached, submachine gun trained on us, demanding in Russian that we identify ourselves. Halfway through the judge's explanation, the soldier cut him off and ordered us to return to Osijek before he took us into custody. We high-tailed it out of there.

Unlike Bulgaria, Croatia drew benefit from its proximity to Slovenia, the most liberal and wealthy of the republic's semi-autonomous states, and the Adriatic Sea. Its judges and courts were less encumbered by the straitjacket of Soviet bureaucracy, hence more flexible and receptive to change. When I met with him, Chief Justice Milan Vuković expressed support for court system reform and modernization. Among other topics, we discussed the importance of periodic judicial conferences to establish and cement judicial solidarity. (A year later, he wrote that he'd organized Croatia's first judicial conference.) At the end of our meeting, he expressed intense concern spawned by mass atrocities perpetrated by the Serb-controlled Yugoslav People's Army and militia against Croatian civilians and paramilitary troops in the ongoing war. He illustrated his narrative with over a hundred color photographs depicting corpses subjected to unspeakable crimes of abuse and torture, speculating on what justice mechanisms might be deployed at the war's end to secure justice for these victims.

My encounter with him launched my exposure to a rule of law dimension unlike routine civil, criminal, family, and administrative caseloads. The encounter also oriented me to future projects I would be privileged to join in states plagued by mass atrocities and genocide, such as Rwanda and Liberia, and in the U.N. International Criminal Tribunal for the Former Yugoslavia, and the hybrid Extraordinary Chambers of the Courts of Cambodia, the Khmer Rouge genocide tribunal.

Water Buffalo on the Landing Strip

In 2002, I was invited to post-genocide Rwanda to speak at its First International Conference on Legal Reform and Law Revision. On arrival, darkness was falling over the sprawling capital of Kigali as Sabena Flight 465 descended through 5,000 feet. I'd been flying for nearly 20 hours, not including layovers. When the pilot announced that the tower had cleared our flight for landing, I sighed relief and turned to the window. Kigali's airport sits on a flat rise, slightly above the surrounding city perched on gently rolling hills. Flashing signal lights marking the tarmac slowly emerged. Kigali's city lights cast a quiet yellow glow over the darkening landscape. Because Rwanda then ranked among the world's poorest countries, access to municipal power was available only in the largest towns and cities. At night, impoverished African cities corroborate their status by the sporadic manner in which they are illuminated, random patches of flickering light here and there with modest levels of traffic casting solitary beams of light that worm through the darkness. The encroaching night was calm and clear, and the plane held steady as we descended through the last thousand feet.

Without warning, the aircraft's engines roared to full throttle, and the plane suddenly swept back up, veering into a wide curve away from the airport. The captain announced that he'd aborted touchdown because of visible runway obstructions. After a broad sweep beyond the perimeter of city lights, he eased the huge jet around and back toward the airport. Again, he announced we'd been cleared to land. Two hundred yards from touchdown, the plane shuddered again as the captain accelerated upward and off to the left, prompting some passengers to cry out in fear. The captain, not without frustration, informed us that the runway remained visibly obstructed. He took the aircraft up several thousand feet and away from the airport.

Some 15 minutes later, the plane again was cleared to land. We collectively sighed when the aircraft came to a stop. The poorly ventilated baggage retrieval area brimmed with passengers on the warm July evening, yielding a rich feast of scent and odor that stretched our capacity to smell, so guarded in our own country between air fresheners, filtered air conditioning, and the daily ritual of deodorizing oneself. And we had opportunity to savor it all as checked luggage leisurely disgorged onto and traveled the belt. The impatience of brooding western males clad in Levi's and nondescript shirts, with thinning hair and sallow complexions, stood in stark contrast to the ebullience of the bright-eyed, sparkling coal-black Rwandan women, many dressed in brightly colored fabrics, rejoicing in each other's company. It occurred to me that we condescendingly refer to them as third world. There is more than one type of third world.

The conference culminated in reform recommendations, which a small contingent of us presented to President Paul Kagame, the Rwandan Chief of State. His response was positive and encouraging. Five months later, the State Department invited us back. This time our mission was to build on those recommendations, to assess judiciary-training requirements, and to review what process-improvement strategies and programs were needed.

Rwanda's system of criminal justice was dealt a nearly fatal blow in 1994 when, over 100 days, burgeoning ethnic unrest culminated in the brutal genocidal slaughter of nearly one million, largely Tutsi residents, the plundering of government institutions, and the collapse of civil order. With a population of around seven million, approximately one out of every seven Rwandans was brutally slain.

In 1996–97, after the fledgling government debated and passed the law for the trial and punishment of those responsible for the genocide, tens of thousands of suspects were apprehended. By May of 1997, 65,976 were incarcerated, and by July of the same year, the number imprisoned had swelled to 112,000. The vast majority remained in pretrial custody in 2002 as the impoverished country sought to rebuild its criminal justice system. The inmate capacity of Rwanda's national detention centers in 1994 was 18,000. It had since been increased by over 30,000, but still dramatically incapable of adequately housing the existing detainee population. Of greatest concern was the detention of women, adolescents, and children accused of having taken part in the slaughter.

Conditions in these severely overcrowded prisons, several of which we assessed, were substandard at best. With 70% of Rwandans surviving at an economic level defined as absolute poverty, government resources were insufficient to adequately feed and care for the large detainee population. In spite of massive international aid, targeting the immediate crisis of caring for hundreds of thousands languishing in border-state refugee camps and Rwandan IDP centers, poor hygiene, rape, and lesser crimes were common; diseases, including AIDS, and malnutrition were widespread in these detention facilities.

Unlike the Holocaust which featured orchestrated mass murder within a highly organized institutional framework, the

Rwandan genocide was occasioned by mass social chaos, uncontrolled violence, brazen assassinations, and political upheaval that incapacitated and culminated in the looting and destruction of the government infrastructure.

Between April and July 1994, the Rwandan judiciary shrank from over 750 to fewer than 244 judges; some participated in the slaughter, then escaped to Zaire, now the DRC; others were victims; many fled to neighboring Uganda, Burundi, or Tanzania. The court clerk population plunged from 214 to 59, leaving many courts without staff. The ranks of prosecutors dropped more precipitously, from 87 to 14, and investigators, from 193 to 39, leaving the prosecutorial system functionally incapacitated. The number of lawyers remaining to service a population of seven million was 19. Of the detainees in custody at the time, the Rwandan government estimated that one-third had no case file, largely because no operative police or prosecutorial system was in place to process and charge them when apprehended.

The effort to restructure the justice system began with the appointment of a new minister of justice assigned to an office in a one of many government buildings in ruins, with files and archives vandalized. Paper was scarce, office equipment, furniture, telephones, and supplies had been looted. With a teeming pretrial detention population exceeding 100,000, the government was reconstructing its criminal justice system.

Because of Rwanda's modern history of cataclysmic ethnic conflict, spawned by German and Belgian imperialism; because the eviscerated justice system was slowly being rehabilitated; and because Tutsi largely populated senior levels of the post-genocidal government, the international community was skeptical of the country's ability to impartially bring to justice, those responsible for planning and orchestrating the slaughter.

In November 1994, the U.N. Security Council authorized creation of the International Criminal Tribunal for Rwanda (ICTR). By July of 1995, the ICTR officially began to function in Arusha, Tanzania. In 2016, the ICTR completed its work and closed its doors after expending hundreds of millions of dollars to prosecute and adjudicate charges brought against a small alliance of senior genocide architects and conspirators. While operational, the ICTR indicted 95 and convicted 61 individuals,

38 of whom remain imprisoned, 20 of whom have completed their sentences, and three of whom died in custody. Its judges acquitted 14 of the accused and transferred cases against 10 defendants to national court systems.

Against this backdrop and with a fraction of the resources consumed by the ICTR, the Rwandan government rebuilt its criminal justice system, processing tens of thousands of those charged with lesser but serious atrocity crimes. Shortly after our arrival, we scheduled visits to courts, interviews with judges and court staff, meetings with the Minister of Justice and other prosecutorial officials and police, and visits to the National Judicial Education and Training Center, and Kigali's Gikondo Prison.

Faced with the urgent need for functional criminal justice machinery, the government struggled to reconstitute its former judicial population of 700 judicial officers. The qualified candidate pool was tiny, forcing improvisation; only 10% of the new appointees had the equivalent of a legal education. Others had university degrees in non-law majors, and many had only a secondary or primary education. Developing a training plan to address these deficiencies was a challenge for our small group, but we were invigorated by the enthusiasm, vision, and determination conveyed by government officials.

Courthouses in Rwanda are simple structures. During our site visits, neither security equipment nor officers were visible at the entrances. The courthouse in Gitarama, a mid-size city west of Kigali, illustrates the informality. As we drove into the dirt parking lot, a small goat on the courthouse porch sauntered inside. We noticed it wandering in the lobby, then strolling into a courtroom. A criminal trial was in process with the prisoner, clad in the pink pretrial detainee pajamas, addressed a panel of three robed judges from one podium. No one paid attention to the goat. The courtroom brimmed with Rwandans. The judges, during our subsequent interviews, lamented having little in the way of legal research materials or decisions from the higher courts to further their understanding of applicable jurisprudence.

Continuing our fact-finding, we interviewed the warden of Kigali's central prison. He then led us onto the stage of a large covered hall in which several hundred detainees, male and female, with shorn heads and dressed in pink pajamas, were quietly seated. All had been charged with various crimes relating to the genocide. He first asked us to address them, explaining our purpose, then permitted three of them to explain to us why they were there. The accounts were incredibly troubling. One male expressed enormous frustration, noting his detention already spanned eight years without a courtroom appearance. He had confessed to prosecutors his role in the genocide but had neither been sentenced nor permitted access to defense counsel. All he wanted was to make good his debt to society and return to his family and former life as a subsistence farmer. Tens of thousands with similar accounts languished in Rwanda's prisons.

Cognizant of these human rights violations, Rwanda's government undertook a risk-fraught experiment in transitional justice to expedite the processing of pretrial detainees. Except for the gravest violators, prosecutors would transfer those who voluntarily confessed their crimes to the jurisdiction of Gacaca Courts, an indigenous justice mechanism deployed much earlier in Rwanda's political history. The accused would appear in their hometowns and villages at open forums presided over by elected village elders briefly trained by justice ministry officials. Appointed as Gacaca judges and serving in panels, they reviewed case evidence, heard detainees confess their crimes, offered locals the opportunity to challenge or comment on those confessions, then consulted on appropriate sentences.

Sentencing was oriented toward reintegrating defendants, wherever possible, into their communities and creating conditions that would enable them to eventually return to productive lives. Seated on the ground in a field, we observed a Gacaca Court in session, listening to local villagers recounting memories of the genocidal horror. The orderly, respectful, and transparent proceedings inspired hope that Rwandans could reconcile themselves to this aberrant chapter in their history and move on. Over the years, the Gacaca system was operative, tens of thousands of defendants languishing in crowded prisons appeared before Gacaca forums, had their cases adjudicated, and completed their sentences. It was an imperfect but grand social experiment in locally dispensed justice with maximum transparency, an experiment that no other post-genocidal or mass-atrocity state has come close to replicating.

Relearning How to Wade

Early on the morning of 17 January 2013, I awoke in my downtown Jakarta hotel to the drum of heavy rain on the windows driven by turbulent gusts. In 2010, I had joined the four-year Indonesian USAID C4J Project as an advisor and consultant. January crests Indonesia's seasonal monsoon, and an unprecedented succession of storms by mid-month had already poured more rain into Jakarta's streets than in all of January 2012. I had scheduled an interview at 8:00 a.m. with the Director General of Indonesia's nearly 400 general-jurisdiction courts. The ten-minute walk through undulating sheets of rain, whipped by gusts from the hotel to our office on the 34th floor of UOB Plaza, notwithstanding an umbrella, drenched my suit. Four of us crowded into a compact cab for the 15-kilometer drive to the Badilum. By now, Jakarta's streets were flooding; we plowed channels through 12-inch deep moving water, fearful that the small vehicle would stall.

After a friendly but intense interview, we searched for a cab. The driver told us his only option was a circuitous route over Jakarta's elevated highways because so many local streets were flooded; in some northern sectors, floodwaters reached three meters above normal levels. We crawled along, averaging five kilometers per hour, for three and a half hours over those highways. Road shoulders were littered with cars that ran out of gas, overheated, or pulled off so occupants could relieve themselves. Our driver dropped us off a quarter mile from the office. The streets were flooded, so we removed our shoes, rolled up our trousers, and sloshed through knee-deep, dirty, and trash-laden flood waters laced with raw sewage.

Our office building lobby, a modern skyscraper in the financial sector, was inundated with three feet of water. The fast-flowing floodwaters had surged unimpeded into the basement and underground parking areas, picking up and slamming vehicles into each other, eventually submerging the entire substructure. Two custodial staff were trapped and lost their lives. Power to the elevators, lights, office equipment, and air-circulation system flickered and died.

A co-worker from the office walked down 34 flights in a dark, oxygen-depleted stairwell, carrying our laptops. Once we had them in hand, a colleague and I set out for the hotel. This time, we kept on our shoes. Within seconds, the churning brown water was up to our waists. Halfway to the hotel, we dropped a foot from the sidewalk, down onto the street, the swirling rising current now up to my chest, my arms extended over my head to keep my laptop dry.

The hotel itself, perched on a rise, was dry, but surrounded like an island by a fast-moving river of trash- and raw sewage-infested floodwater on all sides. Fortunately for me, the hotel's power grid and Internet had not been interrupted, so after a long, hot, soapy shower, I could resume work.

Comprising over 8,000 islands in an extended archipelago, 922 of which are permanently inhabited by indigenous groups speaking over 700 languages, Indonesia ranks among the world's most challenging countries to effectively govern. My first assignment called for an assessment of the prosecution system's costly multi-year effort to automate criminal case processing, and what the system-wide cost impacts were of its chronically substandard performance. My second assignment was to research and craft policy recommendations for restructuring the judicial self-governance and administration framework of Indonesia's complex court system, management oversight of which rests with its supreme court. That management responsibility imposes significant administrative burdens on its justices, diverting time and energy better spent on building a systematic and coherent jurisprudence on which lower court judges could rely.

Exploring Monrovia's Looted Temple of Justice

In early 2005, the USDOJ Office of Prosecutorial Development, Assistance, and Training (OPDAT) dispatched a six-person team to assess Liberia's justice system. The impetus was a letter from Liberian Chief Justice Henry Reed Cooper to U.S. Chief Justice William H. Rehnquist. In his 16 February 2004 letter, Cooper describes Liberia as "… emerging from an extended civil upheaval that has taken its toll on all facets of our society and governmental institutions. The Judiciary was not spared. We need assistance in the rebuilding process." The letter goes on to request assistance from the United States' judiciary to "… provide needed capacity building."

I was privileged to serve on that team with a federal trial judge, two veteran USDOJ prosecutors, a USDOS INL administrator, and a USAID Africa Specialist. The U.S. Embassy in Liberia dictated that the review would be limited, for security purposes, to justice-sector facilities in Monrovia; travel to hinterland cities in Liberia's bush country, in regions infested with armed rebel guerillas, posed too great a risk. I immediately asked embassy officials to reconsider, arguing that an assessment confined to Monrovia could not respond meaningfully to Justice Cooper's request. Eventually, the embassy negotiated an agreement with the United Nations Mission in Liberia (UNMIL) that enabled our team to travel by vintage U.N. Ukrainian helicopters to Greenville, Gbarnga, Zwedru, and Voinjama, where we would be under the protection of U.N. Civilian Police (CIVPOL) and U.N. peacekeeping forces. Not negotiable was the embassy's insistence that we be accommodated in housing within its secured perimeter, that we take our meals in its canteen, and that we not leave the embassy without armored transportation and a plainclothes Marine security detail.

For two weeks in early 2005, our team interviewed a variety of justice-sector officials including Minister of Justice Kabineh Muhammed Ja'neh, a former general of Liberians United for Reconciliation and Democracy (LURD), Chief Justice Cooper and his Supreme Court colleagues, UNMIL officials, lower court judges and administrators, prison officials, bar president, defense counsel, CIVPOL, and local police and citizens.

The American Colonization Society conceived Liberia as an African sanctuary to which former slaves could return. Founded in the early 1800s, its capital city, Monrovia, was named after President Monroe. At the time of our assessment, Liberia was emerging from a ruinous and violent civil war perpetrated by Libyan-trained Charles Taylor and his guerilla insurgents who laid to waste this small country. Taylor's terror regime helped pioneer the kidnapping of youth and their transformation into child soldiers. Once captured, they were subjected to a brutal psychological regimen, designed to convert them into mindless paramilitary rebels, poised to commit unspeakable acts of gratuitous violence when ordered by their adult mentors, in a bond of complete submission.

Taylor and his lieutenants honed these child soldiers to almost mechanically perpetrate such acts even against their own family members. When traveling Monrovia's perimeter roads, we would encounter scores of them sitting idly on the shoulders, their scowling eyes vacantly following our vehicles. UNMIL officials paid them to surrender their weapons, but the poorly funded government, rife with corruption, had no jobs, transitional therapy, or occupational training to salvage these young souls.

When we toured Monrovia's iconic Temple of Justice that housed Liberia's Supreme Court and lower courts, it had been looted of its furnishings, equipment, porcelain bathroom fixtures, and copper wiring. Most windows had been broken or pilfered. The plumbing system was compromised, so every morning, clerical staff would fill buckets at a nearby well and deliver water by hand to offices, chambers, restrooms, and courtrooms on six floors. Access to power was limited; when we met with Chief Justice Cooper and his colleagues on the sixth floor one very warm day, the only ventilation came from two old wheezing desk fans. Several years later, USAID provided funds to restore the Temple of Justice.

As I had anticipated, conditions in the hinterland towns were wretched. Driving through them in CIVPOL SUVs over pocked clay roads, we observed blown-up and burned-out police stations, courts, and jails. At a satellite police station with a dirt floor in Gbarnga in Bong County, I asked the constable where he detained suspects. He opened an adjacent door with 'Police Cell' signage that exposed a small windowless closet. Two juveniles perched on two worn tires in the closet, waiting for a judge to schedule a plea hearing.

We toured a courthouse where the case filing system comprised a cardboard box in a bathroom whose fixtures had been ripped out and stolen. The courtroom was devoid of furniture, except for a single small wooden bench. The judge had no legal or procedural codes. Neither he nor the clerk had been paid in two years; they subsisted from fees and fines imposed by the court. The clerk delivered summonses and subpoenas in person on foot, because no funds were available for gasoline for his small personal motorbike. Delivering a summons or subpoena might take one or more days given the distance to be walked.

Without a court operating budget, paper and pen were in chronically short supply. For jury trials, the clerk would post a notice at the courthouse entrance, then recruit jurors off of adjacent streets for the trial. In lieu of payment for jury service, many negotiated bribes from the litigants for their votes. Toward the end of our visit, we interviewed Charles Gyude Bryant, Chairman of the Transitional Government of Liberia, who invited us to his home that evening for drinks and hors d'oeuvres. Negotiating the ring of surly plain-clothed guards swarming his modest home gave us pause, but the discussion was stimulating until he dozed off, and we quietly made our way out.

The absence of a functioning justice system in the hinterlands, prompted many local chiefs to rely on indigenous practices, deploying trial by ordeal where evidence was in question. Persons accused might be required to (i) drink a poisonous sassywood potion; (ii) have a fiery hot machete pressed against a bared leg; or (iii) reach bare-handed into a bowl of searing hot palm oil to retrieve a submerged palm kernel. If, after doing so, there were no adverse consequences, such as severe gastric illness, or visible signs of severe burns such as broken red skin or blistering, the accused would be declared innocent. The appearance of such adverse consequences was indicative of guilt. In our interview with then-Minister of Interior H. Dan Morias, he expressed support for trial by ordeal when administered by village high priests.

Summing things up

These narratives illustrate the enormous range of complex challenges and the broad scope that effective rule of law work encompasses. Select other notable projects in which I was privileged to participate, include:

> ➢ Working with a small team of senior Iraqi judges in Baghdad's Rusafa Courthouse to rewrite the country's criminal procedure code;
> ➢ Conducting a three-month-long U.N.-sponsored assessment of court management at the Extraordinary Chambers of the Courts of Cambodia, the Khmer Rouge genocide tribunal on the outskirts of Phnom Penh;
> ➢ Leading a small team of international experts advising the justice minister, chief justice, and judicial leaders on crafting a high-level strategic plan for restructuring and modernizing the Kingdom of Saudi Arabia's judicial system;
> ➢ Implementing, with two judges and a law professor, a two-week training curriculum on judging in a democratic society for groups of 50 senior Iraqi judges and prosecutors at Prague's CEELI Institute;
> ➢ Serving as a member of the Abu-Dhabi Government Restructuring Committee and managing the one-year commercial court modernization project; and
> ➢ Serving as interim chief of court management for five months at the U.N. International Criminal Tribunal for the Former Yugoslavia in The Hague.

In each instance, I collaborated with international colleagues and local leaders. As in any human enterprise, levels of commitment, tolerance for corruption, personal integrity, competence, and self-interest varied widely. In each instance, those of high integrity and commitment to the quest for justice and the rule of law gradually emerged. To the extent that my work has been taken seriously by those leaders, it is a function of having invested considerable time to absorb material on how their systems evolved, are structured, governed, and operated. This investment occurred in three segments: first, prior to departing for the assignment; second, during the engagement; and third when compiling the assessment results and formulating recommendations oriented toward fostering sustainability and accountability.

My analyses frequently reach beyond the confines of the court and judicial systems, to explore relationships with the executive and legislative or parliamentary powers, and the extent to which they exercise authority over the judicial power. I research the type and frequency of formal interaction between judicial system leaders and their executive and legislative power counterparts. The variances I have discovered range broadly.

A clear trend is that the less frequent the inter-branch communication, the greater the distrust, suspicion and even contempt. Where I deem it important, I will meet with elected legislators responsible for judicial power oversight. I also meet, where appropriate, with justice and interior ministers to discuss their relations with and posture vis-à-vis judicial system leaders. Determining these relationships is invaluable to grasping inter-branch dynamics. In Liberia, we met with senior officials of the Central Bank of Liberia. Attitude also is a core element. Being modest and unpretentious always trumps flaunting hubris, condescension, and arrogance. And dogmatic persistence in exporting solutions from one's own country, frequently results in failure over the duration.

Markus Zimmer at a training program for Iraqi judges.

Chapter 6
Human Development
Attorney Thanaa El Shamy

My name is Thanaa El Shamy. I am Egyptian. I am working as a Legal Expert. For a long time, I have worked in human development, building a career that is specialized in the legal field in several development projects. Most of these projects in our developing countries are usually funded by donating organizations.

I have worked in projects funded by the European Union, the United Nations as well as European governments working independently such as the Netherlands, Belgium, Denmark, and Germany. I also worked on projects funded by USAID. Mostly, I used to provide legal assistance to those who needed such assistance. Other projects offered legal awareness to the target groups. This has had a great impact on groups of people who are exposed to some problems without having the financial ability to resort to courts or the cognitive ability to understand their problems in order to be resolved. Therefore, these projects used to help them get the required legal and cognitive support.

Throughout all projects where I worked, and what has pleased me the most, in terms of its impact on its beneficiaries, was the Family Justice Project, which began in February 2006. The project was funded by the USAID, under the D&G sector (Democracy and Governance), in collaboration with the Egyptian Ministry of Justice and the National Council for Motherhood and Childhood. This project was planned to be implemented within 5 years, but it was extended in terms of duration and specialization and ended in November 2011. It could have been extended to a longer period, but Egypt has been going through tough circumstances after the January 2011 revolution and the succession of governments which prompted many projects to stop working until the vision gets clearer.

The project was divided into two tasks, the first one worked with the Ministry of Justice on developing family courts and raising the efficiency of its staff, and the second task worked with the National Council for Motherhood and Childhood. Its purpose was to become a communication hub with civil society organizations to help the community in acknowledging the role of the family courts, and to facilitate resorting to them, since the Family Courts Act was still new at that time. Since its issuance in March, 2004, the act has developed a new system of litigation in family issues, promoting a settlement before filing the lawsuit, as a condition for acceptance of family lawsuits. As a result, however, it created a lot of misunderstanding and even rejection of some of the lawyers who questioned the capacity of Mediation Offices staff and argued that this settlement stage prolonged litigation and disrupted proceedings.

It seems to me a more likely reason for rejection by the lawyers, for the idea of a settlement before resorting to the court is that this will reduce their income, where mainly, they rely directly on lawsuits through litigation and they do not have the culture of a lawyer for settling disputes. Consequently, it was inevitable to work with these lawyers to explain the mediation idea and to clarify it as a way of dealing with contested issues without losing their filed cases yield.

During the project, I have worked as a legal expert with the two tasks and I was responsible for the third section, which was added to the project, which will be explained later in this chapter.

We have started the work in three selected governorates representing different sectors of the Egyptian society (Upper Egypt, coastal cities and the Delta); namely Minya, Port Said, and Giza. Minya is a conservative governorate, agriculture is considered its main income. Also, it includes some quarries of iron and steel, sand, and marble, and the Minya population is 3,686,000.

Port Said is a free zone governorate over the Mediterranean Sea, which depends on trading, and the Suez Canal starts from it. Its population is 603,787.

Giza is the 2nd capital of Egypt, a civilized governorate which includes some agriculture on its borders. The Giza population is 7,398,000.

The Action Plan has been to develop family courts in those governorates, develop their employees, and raise the efficiency of non-governmental organizations workers in the same three governorates. As well as introduce them to family law and develop a way to suit the case that requires recourse, to a settlement attempt before resorting to court, and regarding this pilot project as a model to be circulated to the rest of the governorates of Egypt.

Before the work started, we decided to visit these Governorates to identify the needs of those courts' staff, whether they were training needs or their offices development needs, and to provide them with the devices that would help them perform their jobs easily, which leads to perfecting their work from both the quantity and quality aspects, efficiently and smoothly.

It was a whole new experience, since it was my first time to participate in such type of a survey. The Family Justice Project (FJP) has visited all the 17 family courts in the three governorates, where we met with the mediation offices employees. We gave them the survey forms and helped them to understand their content.

The staff interaction was great and their happiness was more than we expected, because the survey form had seriously considered the smallest detail of their work, such as places to meet visiting parties. Since they applied this law quickly, there were no private places for the mediation meetings. Accordingly, the mediation meetings in the beginning were made in the public offices, until FJP renovates what they consider a private meeting room in each office, with a round table only for the mediation meetings which were not available from the beginning since the Act was passed and implemented in a brief period without taking into account the requirements of applying the law.

Based on the survey results, FJP has managed to equip all the mentioned mediation offices of those courts, in the pilot phase, with all requirements requested by the staff; including, but not limited to: legal libraries, furnishing meeting rooms for disputing parties, providing computers, as well as renovation of offices and restrooms in order to be adequate for their needs.

Then we prepared the scientific materials for the training, which included their requested needs, such as training on how to use the computers, in addition to identifying the required documents for each case. Moreover, how to control the situation in case of an erupting clash between the disputing parties that resort to the family courts for mediation. Furthermore, how to write reports that help the trial judge in the case of mediation failure.

After finishing the renovation phase of the mediation offices of the courts, we started preparing for the training, seeking the expertise of psychologists, social specialists, and legal experts to train these employees and consolidate their idea of mediation. We explained the role which the mediation specialist should play in terms of helping the parties suggest their solutions, without the former intervention by expressing any personal opinion. We train them how to congregate the conflict parties and to assist them on demonstrating their problem and give all possible legal solutions so the conflict parties can choose their suitable plan.

After trainings started, we found that it had a great impact on their performance, according to the audience's opinion and the achieved results by comparing the number of cases they helped in mediation before resorting to the courts. This has helped in reducing the pressure on courts and helped judges accomplish the cases before them in lesser time. Also, it has helped the family law to be enforced, through understanding the importance of resorting to mediation and considering it the perfect way to resolve family disputes.

We have started collective training for the mediation team, followed by focused training for each specialty, where the mediation team consists of a social specialist, a psychologist, and a legal specialist. There were special trainings specialized for the social and psychological specialists, in addition to further training for the legal specialist.

The training transformed into a practical form through role-playing, division into working groups and the trainees' interaction was really impressive. Phase one, or the project's pilot phase, was concluded by equipping the pilot governorates' courts and training their staff.

Because of the pilot phase success, the Ministry of Justice has requested dissemination of the same project throughout the rest of the governorates nationwide, but due to the limited budget, it was agreed that only training the mediation offices staff of all family courts, in all the governorates of Egypt, will take place and offices renovation will be postponed.

Training the judges was one of the most sensitive issues, not only to be tackled at the first place but to be implemented as well, because the project is funded by a foreign entity. But due to the great success of training the mediation offices staff, the Ministry of Justice has approved training for all family court judges of the courts of Egypt. This was considered a huge event, since no previous project has managed to train this number of judges. The preparation for this training required lot of time and effort to be appropriate enough, especially when related to the covered topics and even the trainers themselves.

The training has been more than effectively done by the judges of the Court of Cassation and senior judges of the appellate court, with discussion groups discussing controversial issues between judges as well as provisions of the Court of Cassation. Psychology and Management Professors' assistance was sought for training on time management, working under pressure and dealing with difficult patterns. During the training, we started to give the judges a role, playing with different cases and they showed their interest by discussing the cases and the way of solving it together, debating, sharing their opinions, and perspectives as if it was a real case. The judges' interaction was so great that the Ministry of Justice asked for training repetition for three consecutive years, with a new addition every year of printed materials for some of the provisions and emphasis on certain topics as per the judges' request.

The judges were also introduced to the real role of the mediation team, as well as informing them about the trainings the teams have received, and the possibility of the former benefiting from the reports the latter submits in case of mediation failure. Unfortunately, the judges themselves used to have a wrong impression that the mediation process that takes place in court is not serious enough. We even asked the judges to specify certain points that may benefit them in the mediation lawsuit report. The Judges asked the mediations to provide them with the following information:

- Who from the conflict parties has attended by himself, delegated his lawyer, or didn't attend completely?
- Who was refusing any of the provided solutions?

Thus, we trained the mediation team on these points in order to result in a coherent litigation process. We have succeeded in changing the judges' perception and improving the mediation team performance, to the extent that the judges used to seek their help for clarifying certain issues contained in the claims that have not been settled. The Minister of Justice has opened the first round of training sessions, which gave importance to the training and contributed to the obligation of judges to attend all training sessions, raising the degree of benefit from these training courses.

During this project, because of its success and the praise of the Ministry of Justice, a third component has been added to the project, which is the legal aid offices. The Family Law, which was issued in 2004, added a previous step of the litigation, which is the mediation. Mediation relieved litigants, in certain issues, from resorting to a lawyer, and allowed the litigants themselves if they wanted to proceed in those suits, since the start of the suit, without a lawyer. But due to legal illiteracy rampant in the Egyptian society, even among the educated, it was difficult for the disputing parties to follow up with their claims on their own. So we thought with the Ministry of Justice, to establish one or more offices in each of the family courts for legal aid based on the number of court visitors.

We began implementing the idea by determining the quality of staff of those offices and their specialization; we decided that they should be graduates of the law faculties, yet not working in the advocacy career, so their work wouldn't interfere with the legal aid. We also hired computer administrators and required all staff to be graduates, so they wouldn't have previous experiences that conflict with the idea of legal aid.

`We developed the personal characteristics of the employees who would be selected, as well as the degree of excellence in their specialties, and the sympathy they have towards poor people, as if they are doing a charity.

We also started developing the training plan and curriculum for these employees, in order to create a government employee who held special attributes that were not previously available in government staff. The idea was to assist employees to work on a job as if they were public voluntary workers.

After the staff selection in accordance with what was agreed upon, they were divided into groups. Each group experienced a 15-day training camp which included training on all subjects pertaining to legal assistance in personal lawsuit claims. For instance, they learned ways to file a case and ways of writing money orders for minors who are under guardianship; also ways to familiarize them with required documents for each suit. This information would help them to present complete documents to the judge, and thus, reduce litigation time. They were trained as well on how to receive audiences (interviewing people), deal with their difficult patterns (mentally retarded people), and who has the feeling of persecution. Their job description within the office was established, to allow one employee to escort the legal aid seeker, to facilitate the procedures of the suit in the rest of the court offices.

We have also assisted the Ministry of Justice in developing models for suit claims and orders, which were installed on computers to facilitate the work of those offices and prevent errors that may disrupt the proceedings.

During the staff groundwork, we have prepared legal aid offices inside the court buildings by choosing the right place for the office, preparing and furnishing it, equipping it with necessary appliances for staff work and preparing waiting areas for the public. We have also supplied the offices with paper and electronic legal libraries.

We have also met with family courts judges and workers who shall deal with legal aid staff, to explain the role of employees in these offices and how to assist those who resort to them in writing case reports, determining the hearing, and implementing the judges' requests during the course of the lawsuit. They have been helped in implementation of the rule after the end of the lawsuit. These offices played a major role in public service and facilitating the work of the judges due to presenting comprehensive reports and documents.

After the completion of the offices work, we prepared a manual to train employees in mediation offices, which included the necessary practical material to train new employees, and another manual on preparing legal aid offices, with tools and books in order to ensure the completion of legal aid offices with the rest of the courts.

The FJP project had the biggest influence, from my own perspective, in developing family courts, increasing the efficiency of mediation specialists, and making a module for the facilities of the offices, so it can be generalized. In addition, correcting the misunderstanding about the role of mediation offices for many people, including lawyers and judges, lay the foundation of legal aid offices in family court to assist a big sector of disabled people.

As for the department, which worked with civil society, it has also been worked with the same three pilot governorates of Minya, Port Said and Giza only, without extending to the rest of the governorates nationwide. This department was intended to explain the family law and to facilitate dealing with it by the target groups through NGOs. Therefore, some NGOs working in the field of family and children were chosen, and trained on the Personal Status Law and understanding its updated stages to make it easier for them to explain it for those who deal with them in the scope of their organizations.

Basically, there was a lack of understanding of the law by the public and by those whose problems require going to court or to mediation. Also, there was resistance from lawyers who incited litigants not to go for the mediation on the grounds that it delays the lawsuit.

We have helped the organizations (NGOs) to do trainings for lawyers to change their point of view regarding the mediation process and its importance before resorting to court. In addition, we provided comprehensive explanation of the law and its importance to the public by training courses for young lawyers.

We searched for those who would have a great impact and a strong influence within the community, in order to spread legal awareness.

We found that in the Eastern societies, the most influential people are the clerics, hence, popped the idea of explaining the family law to clergymen. So, we decided to assemble Muslim and Christian clergymen in groups, and started explaining to them the Family Law and its updated part of the mediation before filing the lawsuit.

We also explained the importance of disputants taking the mediation topic seriously; to the extent of its impact on reducing conflict in the future, spreading the idea of tolerance, forgiveness, and non-violence.

As a legal specialist myself, I played this role despite my fears at the beginning because most of the clerics were older than me. I feared that because of their extensive knowledge and esteemed presence, it would be hard for them to treaty me as a knowledgeable teacher. The combination of Christian and Muslim clerics in one session was such a new concept and experience, to the extent that the American project manager insisted on observing the training to evaluate it.

Thankfully, things went smoothly, in a respectful way that impressed everyone. So, we repeated the experience in all the governorates where the project operated. This offer was met with great welcoming from the clergymen themselves, and they accepted us with understanding, conviction, and friendship that still exist today.

Then we came up with the idea of training young people on the concept of choosing a life partner. The idea was to limit family conflict by making them aware of problems that may result from the wrong choices. We prepared a training manual with the materials on how to choose a life partner, how to deal with children in cases of separation, and treatment of adolescent problems resulting from broken families. Our goal was to limit the number of children who end up on the streets committing robberies, dealing drugs, and engaging in prostitution.

Psychologists and social workers working in NGOs have been trained on how to conduct mediation and family dispute resolution, focusing not necessarily upon returning to married life, but on solving problems; all without resorting to court. We encouraged working within the Personal Status Law.

The participating NGOs in the project have been so successful in resolving family problems, that we have established a new tradition. At the end of each year, we help organizations sponsor an entertaining day of celebration for families who have successfully resolved their disputes.

The project has expanded its role, where some organizations now address problems related to issues such as the phenomenon of destitute families marrying off underage girls to older men from the Gulf countries, for the sole purpose of making money.

So, we held awareness sessions for those families on the health and social risks of underage marriage, on the impact of a child's right to education, and to choose their own spouse. We accomplished that with informative videos and educational films.

The project also addressed and worked on solving another problem: illegal immigration. Including the legal risks and physical dangers of illegal immigration. We also sought to empower families by giving them basic skills necessary to acquire an income that would reduce the risk and dangers to them, and their families, of breaking the law. Without these basic skills, most of these young people would end up being arrested and deported back to Egypt.

Technical and financial support deemed necessary was provided to organizations for training the target groups or to help them accomplish their plans related to law enforcement. Also, education and training on writing project proposals for financial support has been provided for employees in NGOs. This support is essential for expanding the scope of their social work.

The Family Justice Project, which I worked with for nearly six years, was one of the best projects I worked on in my entire career. It provided me with practical skills and life experiences essential in dealing with one of the high-level sovereign ministries in Egypt; namely the Ministry of justice; and I was the responsible person for dealing directly with the ministry.

It is never easy for anyone outside the ministry to access the system and express their opinion regarding the work processes. Dealing closely with the Ministry was the reason I could understand their work system in some cases and even improve it in other cases.

My direct contact with judges and the previous experience of working with women's complaints office (Ombudsman Office) made me aware of the problems faced by the public in litigating in family courts, and enabled me to work on resolving them by putting them on the judges training agenda.

On a personal level, I gained continuous lifetime friendships with judges, university professors and others who have played the role of trainers and training facilitators, especially my direct colleagues in the project, even those who live abroad. We try to meet whenever possible and we are all staying in touch through social media and networking.

Some of these friendships continued even five years after the project was completed, which enriched my life on both the personal and professional levels.

Thanaa El Shamya at an Egyptian training.

Chapter 7
Time Abroad
Justice Joseph Nadeau

As for me, I had the good fortune to work with hundreds of judges, government leaders and in-country specialists; conducting training programs for judges, staff, prosecutors, and defenders in the former Russian Republics, Central and Eastern Europe, the Middle East, and Southeast Asia. The experiences of the authors set out in this book demonstrate the impact of international cooperation.

We in the United States are entering a period when many in power are asking: Why should we care? Can the U.S. really have an impact in these foreign countries? Is it really in our interest to spend this time and these tax dollars abroad? My answer to those questions is unequivocally: Yes.

Let me offer two observations from my experiences from working in countries in transition. First, the purpose of international work is not to change other governments into American democracies, or to turn judicial systems into the American model, but to expose judges and government leaders to important democratic Rule of Law principles. Second, I always learn something new from each program in which I participate abroad.

USAID reaches every country in the world interested in fostering the Rule of Law, with projects and programs to assist all branches of foreign governments to protect human rights and foster social and economic development. I believe it makes a concerted effort to establish staying power, by a program of constant evaluations and system mechanisms designed to promote sustainability.

One of my most memorable USAID experience came in June 2005, when I travelled to Bratislava, Slovakia to work with Iraqi Federal Supreme Court Chief Justice Medhat

Mahmoud and other senior Iraqi judges to develop provisions for the new Iraqi Constitution which would preserve the independence of the judiciary.

Chief Justice Medhat, who has written a chapter for this publication, was appointed supervisor of the Iraq Justice Ministry in June 2003 by U.S. Diplomat Paul Bremer. He then became president of the Federal Appeals Court, and was appointed chief justice of the Supreme Court in March 2005, just three months before the conference. Chief Justice Medhat currently serves as the head of the Supreme Judicial Council which is responsible for oversight of all Iraqi courts.

At our June 2005 conference, Chief Justice Medhat was passionate about addressing the problems facing the Iraqi judiciary, strengthening its independence, protecting the judges and their families, and acquiring suitable facilities in which to conduct court business. He told us the war had destroyed or severely damaged most court buildings and equipment, and the justice system was hampered by negative perceptions of the judiciary as a mechanism of the former regime under Saddam Hussein.

By the time of the Bratislava conference, about twenty percent of Iraqi judges and prosecutors in the Southern region had been removed for corruption or links to the former regime. Between that purge and the tenuous state of security, all Iraqi courts were severely understaffed. Some judges actually slept in the buildings used for courts because of security concerns for the safety of themselves and their families.

We spent the week in large group sessions with presentations and discussions about judicial independence, the role of the judiciary in a democracy, judicial ethics, and a wide range of court planning and management subjects. In two small groups, the judges then worked on drafting new constitutional provisions and developing a strategic plan for discrete tasks to improve the courts that they could implement immediately on their return.

At times, it seemed the Iraqi judges felt the issues facing them were overwhelming and beyond their control. One of the realities we stressed at training conferences was that, in any country, there will be barriers to the things the judiciary want to accomplish, but there will also be opportunities. What we hoped to help them with was identifying those barriers, showing how they could overcome them, and demonstrating how to make the most of the opportunities.

The primary purpose of the conference was drafting recommendations for the new constitution that they could all agree upon. The judges were eager to accomplish that in time to have them conveyed by the chief justice to the drafting committee for presentation to the voters. With the skilful guidance of the chief justice, the Iraqi judges agreed upon fourteen constitutional provisions they believed necessary to strengthen their judiciary and to advance public trust in the judicial branch. They also formed a strategic plan to address their most immediate needs: protection for themselves and their families, suitable buildings in which to work, merit appointment of additional judges, qualified staff for administrative tasks, and the most basic equipment for processing cases. Imagine trying to function with those challenges.

Within a year of our conference, two judges and the Chief Justice's son had been assassinated.

In an email home at the end of the project, I wrote:
This is an amazing group of judges who struggle each day not just to do their jobs, but to protect themselves and their families. Imagine if you needed four guards around the clock just to get to work. Imagine that all you did each day was work, eat, and stay in your home. Sporadic electricity, virtually no contact with the outside world, except for projects like this now underway. It will be impossible to forget who these judges are and what they have done here.

In November 2006, the N.H. Supreme Court Society selected Chief Justice Medhat to receive its first 'Life and Liberty' award, sponsoring his visit to New Hampshire to receive it. At the Supreme Court, to a standing-room only audience, the Chief Justice gave a moving acceptance speech in Arabic with translation by a Phillips Exeter Academy Arabic language teacher. Later in the week, he addressed one thousand students and faculty at an Academy assembly. He told the students that they and the young people in his country would be the ones to insure individual rights and lasting peace. After the assembly, he met with several classes to answer student questions.

It seemed to me that our entire experience with Iraq's Chief Justice and its courts went a long way to fulfill what I believe to the State Department's goal, to support and strengthen key allies and partners and meet global challenges.[i]

At some stage in nearly every foreign judicial training program in which I have been involved, a judge will ask how courts in the United States issue rulings that are honored by government leaders and the people even if everyone disagrees with the decision. My response is always the same: What is essential is the moral imperative of judges, the high motivation of leaders, and a universal respect for the constitution.

One goal of USAID and its trainers was to assist committed judges to achieve and maintain that moral imperative of the rule of law.

An important characteristic of many foreign judiciaries is that their systems are based on the Napoleonic Code, the French civil law system, and not on the common law. Consequently, there is no *stare decisis,* or even printed Supreme Court decisions, for guidance. Legal training is not by case study and Socratic method, but by memorizing statutory provisions. Statutes then, not Supreme Court decisions, form the basis upon which judicial decisions are made. As a result, trial judges do not have precedent to look to when deciding cases. For the most part, the judges just make sure all the paperwork is correct, statutory mandates are followed, and investigations are complete.

Lack of printed precedent also lends more importance to interpretations of laws by Ministries of Justice. Since there is no easy exchange for judicial interpretation of the laws, it is usually the justice ministries that disseminate determinations to judges. Even many foreign supreme courts seemed to render decisions on a case-by-case basis. Many of these supreme courts decide, not only if the laws are followed, but may change results based on their own view of the evidence.

Even though it is not always easy for foreign judiciaries to believe that principles of our judicial practices can be applied to their systems, most foreign judges are eager to learn how our courts function and how they, as judges, can change judicial practices to gain public trust, and as a result, more judicial independence.

My first experience in a USAID program was in Latvia in 1993, a year and a half after it fought for and achieved independence from the Soviet Union, which turned out to be typical of early trainings in emerging democracies.

With an American judicial educator as the program leader and a German trial judge, I prepared and presented a four-day training program for recently named judges on Judicial Independence, Community Relations, Ethics, Media, and the Role of the Judge in an Adversarial System.

This experience is vivid in my memory for many reasons. I discovered quickly that the presentations I had prepared were perfect for new judges … new American judges. It became clear to me that the prior training and experience of these foreign judges had focused upon ministerial tasks, not broad judicial principles. They just were not prepared to engage in the process of critical thinking or equipped with the skills to consider the unique role of judges in modern open societies.

After my initial presentation, I skipped lunch, threw away my prepared talks, and hastily sketched new notes. The fresh presentations were more basic and simplified. I tried to engage the judges in broader discussions of fundamental principles. Unfortunately, the judges were not amenable to that format. They were too accustomed to a structure that consisted of lectures, followed by breaks, followed by more lectures. They were not ready to engage in the group dynamic of interaction and discussion.

It did not help that a representative of the Ministry of Justice, a former Communist party leader, was there to monitor everything that was said. At the end of the first day, in fact, the Minister told us that we could no longer talk about the independence of the judiciary, and if we did, he would end the program. Really.

To lighten things up, we invited the judges to be our guests at lunch. Somehow, that invitation did not get to the ministry guy. This gave us an informal setting for further discussion and led to a more relaxed conversation. The judges were fairly open about their professional lives and the nature of their work. They were clearly intimated by the Ministry of Justice, and not quite sure about judicial independence, but were eager to learn about us.

In all of these emerging democracies, the Ministry of Justice, an executive branch department, was responsible for judicial administration. That meant hiring clerks and staff, assigning and regulating judges, and handling all the usual administrative tasks. Because of this lack of separation of powers, outcomes in cases could be influenced. Uncooperative judges could be reassigned far from home. Staff could be hired as a matter of patronage. Judges had no control of staff because they were subject only to the Ministry of Justice. Appreciating these consequences helps one to appreciate and understand what it really means to have a judiciary free of control by the other branches.

I was surprised to see that over half of the Latvian judges in the program were women. That was truly impressive, until we learned the reasons: judicial positions were not highly sought after, they did not pay well, the judge's role was mostly ministerial, and the judges were often just moved from one clerical job to another. Since most of the clerks were women, most new judges in the lower courts were women as well.

This is how it was twenty years ago, and although I have not been back to Latvia since, I have little doubt things have dramatically changed. In part, I will wager, thanks to the work of USAID and similar organizations from other countries. Countries including Canada, Australia, Great Britain, Sweden, China, and the European Union are also conducting training programs and cultural activities to build strategic relationships with these newly independent states. These countries recognize that it is in their interest for the economies of emerging democracies to flourish, for them to be viable for foreign investment, and that to accomplish those goals, a reliable, well-functioning, incorruptible judicial system is absolutely essential.

During the Latvian training session, I had the opportunity to meet and talk with the Chief Justice of the Latvian Supreme Court. He was concerned about the status of the judicial system and was struggling with the question of how to enhance the independence of the judiciary. He was interested in our thoughts about how he could do that without provoking the parliament into exerting even more control over the courts. At the conclusion of the Latvian program, a young judge was selected by the others to address us. His comments were surprising and touching. This is pretty close to what he said:

When we were told to come to this program, I thought, *What are Americans doing here; what can I possibly learn from them.* But now I know, and I want to thank you for coming; I have learned so much. It is an honor for us that you would take the trouble to be here, and I hope you will come back again.

That sentiment was expressed over and over in my early work with judges from Central and Eastern Europe and the former Soviet Republics. In Albania, I met the new president of the Parliament who had been imprisoned for five years by the previous administration for, according to him, expressing his support for democratic reform, and for his ability to speak English. I said it was an honor to meet him and he said the honor was his that we would come to the aid of his country.

I was in Albania as an American representative, with judges from France and the Netherlands, on a Council of Europe project, working with members of the three branches of the Albanian government to enact legislation establishing a school for the education of judges and prosecutors, modeled after France's Ecole Nationale de la Magistrature. Interestingly, the only female participating in the process was a judge who was to be named Director of the school when it was established. She was very deferential to the other officials during our discussions, leaving me with the impression that was the reason for her selection.

The Chief Justice of Albania was a thinker and a reformer. He believed in the importance of an independent judiciary, the separation of powers, the merit selection of judges, and encouraged continuing judicial education. He was a delight to work with and stayed focused, even though the other branches seemed determined to limit his role in the education process.

As an indication of the fragility of some of these emerging democracies, after adoption of the legislation establishing the school and adoption of a new constitution, the Chief Justice of Albania was told by the President to resign. He asked me to review the constitution and give him my opinion on whether he could be removed. I told him it was clear to me that the constitutional provisions relating to the court grandfathered sitting justices, and the president did not have the authority to remove him. When he refused to resign, he was forcefully removed from office by armed military. So much for early independence. Not unexpectedly, USAID's website reports that since 1992, U.S. aid has helped Albania move from the most isolated and repressive communist state in Europe toward a democracy with a market-oriented economy.

In contrast to the forcible ouster of the Albanian Chief Justice, this year, the Accountability and Justice Commission of Iraq attempted to remove Chief Justice Medhat from office. Purportedly for ties to the former regime. The attempt, although obviously political, was somewhat surprising, as it was well known that the Chief Justice had been in the Iraqi judiciary since 1960. The Chief Justice was reinstated peaceably by an appellate court.

In June 2006, I travelled to Amman, Jordan to take part in the first conference on the Establishment of the Arab Center for Judicial and Legal Studies for 15 Middle Eastern Countries. I gave a presentation on Judicial Conduct and Management of Cases, and participated on panels discussing Media, Judicial Performance, and Ethics. Although most of the judges were Muslim, the focus was on general principles underlying an independent judiciary. Just one conference or even many conferences do not create an independently functioning judiciary however.

I believe there are three characteristics by which to measure judicial independence in any country. First, the process of selecting and retaining judges. Second, the autonomy of the individual judge. Third, the nature of the judicial branch of government.

Of necessity, most selection processes are partisan to some degree, because whether judges are elected or appointed, the party in power tries to find judges who it believes share the party's philosophy. So, an important way to assure that the party in power or a government official cannot determine or control the decision of judges once they are confirmed, is to provide them with long terms, and provisions that they cannot be removed, except by impeachment and conviction for serious misconduct. Judges gain and preserve their moral imperative when they do not let themselves be influenced by public officials, the military, or private inducements, and when the people see that judges cannot be so influenced.

Third, the judicial branch itself must maintain its independence from the other two branches. The Court should be able to hire and train its own court clerks and staff. The courts should be able to adopt its own personnel policies, and to establish a fair process for discipline and removal of employees for incompetence or misconduct. Courts should be responsible for allocating resources. Court buildings should be safe, dignified, and well maintained.

In many countries, however, judicial administrative tasks are the responsibility of an executive department, often the Ministry of Justice, which also has responsibility for prosecutors and corrections. Whether courts are independent under the executive branch administration, then, will depend upon the philosophy and vision of the Minister.

Intervening events in some of these countries demonstrate the fragility of early efforts to establish a truly separate third branch of government.

From work in these and other countries, I learned the importance of making clear that it was not the purpose of USAID to tell judges how to do their jobs or to urge them to adopt our system of justice. We explain that we are in their country to help them understand how the system works for us, and how it might work for them, even though in the U.S. our aspirations are not always met, and our system is not perfect. Our role was to show them how we do things, and to give them comparisons that might help them decide for themselves what was best for their courts.

From 2007 to 2011, I made many trips to consult for the Indonesian Supreme Court. Indonesia, a democratic republic since 1998, suffered from pervasive government corruption following sixty years of dictatorship. Transparency International, the global civil society organization fighting against corruption, reported the country was perceived as the most corrupt in Southeast Asia. Understandably perhaps, the court system had not escaped the corrupt environment.

The Supreme Court made it clear that they did not want 'the usual training' of primarily lecture. Instead, the court sought to have the judges participate in the training and engage with the material. To encourage this, we created video scenarios and re-enactments of situations judges might face. Using professional actors, these scenarios included instances of gift-giving, bribes, delays of proceedings and discipline, impartiality, and threats.

For years, the courts have been plagued by a culture of gift giving and influence peddling. My task was to work with an Indonesian law professor and local staff, to create a training program on a new Judicial Code of Conduct for the country's 6,000 judges. Relying heavily on videos, scenarios, small group discussions, and participant interaction, we trained over 2000 judges in Jakarta, Yogyakarta, Bali, Makassar, Surabaya, Semarang, Bandung, and Serang. The Supreme Court Judicial Training Institute will train the rest using our model and materials.

Indonesia is the third largest democracy, the fourth largest nation in population, and has the largest percentage of Muslims in the world. It has an old, rich, and diverse culture. It has vast natural resources and large agricultural output. The people I met included judges from every province, university students, lawyers, and young professionals. They were warm, industrious, devout, deferential, and peaceful. Indonesians seem more likely to befriend one another than to antagonize one another.

While Indonesians are very protective of their own religion, they are also tolerant of the Christian, Hindu, and Buddhist minorities. It seems unfortunate that most Americans probably first learned about Islam as a result of the outrage of 9/11, and that many of our impressions of the people who practice this religion come from terrorist extremists who certainly do not represent the Muslims I met in my travels.

So, is there a message here? I think so. Judges and people around the world share our hopes, fears, dreams, and sense of family. They appreciate our efforts, they want democracy to succeed, and they are working to make it happen. As with all emerging democracies, there are challenges, obstacles to progress, and setbacks. But the journey continues.

I recently addressed 300 Muslim judges and prosecutors graduating from the Algerian Magistrate School. The Minister of Justice, with whom I worked at a Rule of Law program in 2001, invited me back to Algiers to talk with the new judges about judicial independence.

In Algeria, as in all democracies, an independent judiciary helps protect constitutional rights. Although Islam is the official state religion in this country of forty million, the right to hold individual creeds is protected by the constitution. Judicial philosophy in Algeria is undoubtedly reinforced by principles rooted in religion, as it is in the United States. But the justice system is based upon secular laws enacted by parliament, just as our justice systems are based upon secular laws enacted by legislatures.

During my visit, I talked with people about constitutional rights and religious freedom. There, I witnessed first-hand, the frustration Muslims feel when someone refers to radical extremists as Islamic terrorists. People I met are as outraged as we are by violent extremism. They believe that those claiming to act in the name of Islam have perverted their religion to justify a barbaric delusionary fantasy of world domination. Civilized Muslims do not consider those radical extremists as representing Islam, any more than civilized Americans consider radical extremists who bomb courthouses and clinics as representing Christianity.

In 1987, during the Regan/Gorbachev Cold War era, I travelled to the former Soviet Union. At a program in Armenia, I attended a dinner and sat beside a man who spoke no English. Staring at me frequently during the meal, he suddenly declared, "I, Bolshevik."

I was startled by this apparently anti-American comment. Then, at the end of the meal, he turned to me again, raised his glass, and said, "Viva America."

I have worked for nearly thirty years throughout Central and Eastern Europe, Asia, and the Middle East on Rule of Law programs sponsored by the United States Agency for International Development (USAID). From Algeria to

Indonesia, I have heard people say essentially, again and again, "Viva America."

Individuals are often unhappy with governments: their own or someone else's. But they appreciate and admire Americans who willingly come to their country to share knowledge and to promote universal principles. I always felt that people I met around the world believe Americans represent the best of humanity. And that to them, America is first.

My international experiences do not make me a foreign policy expert, but they have given me personal insight into the importance of American friendship to the people of other nations and to our own nation. If I have learned anything from Rule of Law programs, it is that American exceptionalism and American values are on quiet display whenever we work person-to-person with people from other countries.

Justice Nadeau and Chief Justice Mahmoud at a 2005 conference to draft judicial provisions for the new Iraqi Constitution.

Justice Nadeau with Indonesian District Court judges.

Chapter 8
Switzerland's Experience in Justice Support

Simone Troller, Mila Reynolds

Introduction

Supporting justice sector reform has always been a difficult undertaking for development agencies and donors. It's a highly political sector and engaging in it involves exposure to risks. Justice reform trajectories are far from linear and lasting change is, to a significant extent, dependent on local ownership and reform champions. Success, thus, is far from guaranteed.

The way donors and development agencies have approached justice support has, however, been problematic. Practices of importing and replicating sets of laws and institutions, of pursuing top-down approaches that fail to acknowledge local realities and the obstacles justice users face, and of intervening on the basis of unrealistically short time horizons, have rarely led to desired results.

The Swiss Agency for Development and Cooperation (SDC) has increasingly found itself working in fragile and conflict-affected countries, and as a result, has adopted new strategic approaches to respond to challenges emanating from such contexts. Switzerland equally adopted the New Deal for Engagement in Fragile States (New Deal) in 2011, which identifies justice as one out of five peace- and state-building goals key for achieving development results in these contexts.

As a result of this strategic shift, SDC needs appropriate instruments and approaches for working on justice, especially in these contexts. SDC therefore embarked on an 18-month long learning process that aimed at analyzing and understanding its engagement in the justice sector, at identifying lessons learnt, and at distilling the key criteria conducive for justice support.

Beside the question of how SDC approaches justice sector support, a related question was whether there is a role for a small to mid-size donor with limited political weight to engage in this area. Or in other words, what would be a possible role for a donor like SDC, in a sector that is highly politicized and in which many donors bolster their engagement with their economic and political weight?

The following sections review donor approaches in justice support, explore above questions, and illustrate, including on the basis of Switzerland's programs in Bolivia, SDC justice support.

Common Donor Approaches to Justice Support

Donor engagement in justice support has been thoroughly reviewed by think tanks, academics, and practitioners. The following paragraphs summarize the main characteristics of the justice sector, as well as criticism leveled at donors and development actors as to how they seek change in this field.

There is generally agreement that rule of law strengthening and justice reform is a deeply political process. Rule of law and justice processes determine how disputes about resources or power are being resolved; how power is kept in check and shared; how states are held to account; or how criminal justice is administered. Some groups will benefit from changes in the justice sector, others will lose out. Reform efforts thus generate resistance, not least because they may have a redistributive impact. Despite the clear political nature of justice reform, programs have often remained, in many, respects technical, legalistic, and top-down in nature.

Justice programs have tended to focus on form and formalities rather than on the functions of justice.

For example, development actors have approached reform with a predefined idea of what justice institutions, procedures and laws in a given country should look like, rather than tailoring solutions based on context and existing mechanisms. That also meant that programs defined the solution from the outset (solution-driven) rather than taking a given justice problem as the starting point and identifying home-grown solutions adapted to local realities (problem-driven). Development programs have thus tended to replicate or import models of justice procedures and mechanisms, with, at times, poor local ownership and connection to realities.

That also meant that formalized structures and institutions tended to be favored over informal or customary justice mechanisms. Such approaches are particularly problematic in fragile and conflict-affected contexts, where legal pluralism and the co-existence of multiple legal and customary codes and mechanisms is the norm rather than the exception, and where the role of the state is either significantly limited and/or contested. Approaches that ignore legal pluralism and focus predominantly on formal structures and institutions, tend to be poorly connected to local realities and may not enjoy support by the public.

A common mistake for development actors engaged in justice support, has been the assumption that reform processes are linear and that investments into formal justice systems translate into improved services and outcomes. As a consequence, programs have tended to apply a standard set of interventions (for example developing strategies, policies, manuals, procedures, and delivering trainings). They have also frequently used theories of change, based on the notion that activities and outputs of a clearly technical nature (policy development support, capacity-building, curriculum development, etc.) will result in a more efficient justice system, increased access, or improved human rights protection. In short, programs have tended to ignore the political economy inherent in the sector.

Undertaking a Learning Process

Amid calls by academics, practitioners, and think-tanks, for different approaches to justice reform efforts, SDC undertook a learning process with the aim of providing guidance to all staff and partners, taking into consideration what its own engagement looked like and the key lessons learnt and elements necessary for successful justice sector engagement.

There were two additional strategic reasons for SDC's learning process on its own justice sector engagement. First, justice sector support is becoming more important in international development. This is on the hand due to the greater prominence of justice, rule of law, peace, and human rights in the international development Agenda 2030 (SDG 16 in particular). Second, and as noted above, SDC, like other bilateral development agencies, pays increasing attention towards fragile and conflict-affected contexts. The shift has been institutionalized in the current Dispatch to Parliament 2017–2020, and a key question for SDC, thus, was whether it is equipped to contribute to positive change in fragile and conflict-affected contexts and in a highly political sector.

Findings from the Learning Process

SDC possesses advantages that are conducive for successful justice support. Most importantly, SDC has a strong normative and policy commitment to human rights and the rule of law, which dates back to the 1990s and which underpins its engagement. As a result, SDC justifies rule of law strengthening and justice support as an end in itself and not only as a means to an end (such as economic growth, poverty reduction).

The learning process has shown that the problematic approaches detailed above partially hold for SDC. For example, SDC is not immune to reform approaches that are solution-driven (rather than taking a problem and its context as the starting point) and that draw on a standard set of interventions. SDC, at times, also employs formulaic and standardized theories of change and it has shown a certain comfort with technical approaches (programs that address capacity gaps constitute a large percentage of all programs with justice components). SDC is also slightly more state and institution centered in its engagement, although it has a track record of dealing with customary or non-formal systems.

That said, there is ample evidence that SDC undertakes contextually appropriate programs that are maneuvered in a politically smart way, take into account power dynamics, and use windows of opportunity in a flexible and strategic manner, as the Bolivia example further below illustrates. SDC has also shown its ability to successfully work on justice in restricted political environments. Such engagements are based on thorough context analysis and its capacity to tap into local knowledge and acquire in-depth local expertise. In practice, thus, the learning process has shown that SDC is knowledgeable about the political economy and how to successfully maneuver in such environments.

Important to note is the institutional set-up and decision-making within SDC. Country strategies – agreed upon between country presences and headquarter, and aligned with national development plans, define the main themes of engagement in a given context. Country offices have the overall operational responsibility for programs while headquarter focuses on strategic questions. In other words, country offices enjoy considerable room for maneuver to design, implement, and review programs during their life cycle. While there are platforms and meetings to facilitate knowledge and experience-sharing on given themes among the various offices, the rationale, design, and intervention strategies for programs are initiated by country presences.

Programs thus may grow organically over their lifespan (of usually 2–6 phases of 4 years each), adding or amending components and directions, building upon achievements and lessons learnt, and reacting to new developments and opportunities, without following a blue-print or rigid plan. Key for such a way of managing programs is a long-term perspective when engaging, continuous learning and adjusting, and delegating operational decision-making to actors closest to implementation.

SDC's thematic orientation on justice, similar to that of other donors, varies considerably and addresses very different justice, rights, and accountability issues. SDC works on a broad range of justice themes and sub-themes that include, for example, justice components as part of rural development initiatives (land governance and land conflict prevention), initiatives aimed at curbing gender-based violence, 'traditional' justice programs that work on one or several parts of the justice chain (prosecution, legal reform, etc.) with a strong focus on the correction system. Other programs focus on social protection including legal identity, and others again deal with justice-related issues in the context of migration and forced displacement.

The finding that SDC's justice sector engagement covers such a broad variety of themes, has been met with mixed reactions. Somewhat unsurprisingly, initial reactions within SDC included calls for a more strategic and focused engagement that limits itself to clear areas of thematic expertise. One of the key arguments was that SDC, as a donor, has a limited budget in this sector and thus cannot risk to be spread too thinly. While that call is understandable, it would be wrong to heed it. The multi-dimensional nature of the justice sector is naturally perceived as a challenge to donors, yet embracing this breadth allows for interventions to be designed in a context-relevant and adaptive manner.

Approaching justice not as a sectoral issue but as critical dimension to a development challenge, is more likely to guarantee that an engagement in justice support will focus on the function of justice and on solving actual problems for people. This inevitably implies that programs are not strictly limited to justice sector only, but include other dimensions (be it health, food security, conflict prevention, human rights and protection) and in this way, recognize the multi-dimensional nature of development challenges. And even though SDC's thematic focus is broad, it has a distinct profile with regards to a number of recurring themes: human rights, gender-based violence, criminal justice, and land and property regulations.

Lessons Learnt – Criteria for Successful Justice Support

The learning process has led to a number of important insights. Most importantly, it identified elements that make justice reform more likely to succeed. Several of these are characteristic of SDC's engagement. And while these elements are equally relevant for other sectors, due to the nature of justice support (as a very political undertaking) they are of particular significance for this field.

First, the long-term focus of SDC's engagement ensures the necessary breadth for achieving results. There are hardly any quick fixes in justice support, and given its political nature, it elicits resistance. Change trajectories are most likely uneven and far from linear. Second, SDC's decentralized structure and decision-making processes enhance context-relevance and allow for the design of programs that reflect country needs, socio-political realities, ensure local ownership, and seek to resolve concrete problems.

Delegating responsibility to those closest to operational decision-making enhances the likelihood that programs are designed on the basis of what already exists and do not present a solution up-front on what should be in place. As a matter of fact, many of SDC's programs are not just about justice, but include a significant justice component as one of several dimensions to a development challenge. In other words, programs do not treat justice as a sector isolated from others, and instead, keep a multidimensional focus on the development challenge.

Third, linked to above point, most programming positions within SDC's country offices are nationalized. National staff hold key functions in designing and implementing programs. This set-up allows SDC to understand local power dynamics and the political economy inherent in the section. While national staff is naturally part of that power structure, they are at the same time uniquely placed to understand and interpret local power dynamics. Several international SDC colleagues who have worked on justice affirmed that they would have faced enormous difficulties without national staff's knowledge and expertise.

Regarding the question about SDC's role as a comparatively small donor without strong political weight: Switzerland is generally perceived as a neutral political without a geopolitical agenda. These traits are an advantage when engaging on justice as they may elicit less suspicion. It is also important to note that a larger budget does not increase the likelihood of justice reform success. On the contrary, and as mentioned at the outset of this chapter, local ownership and reform champions will make the difference. And the comparatively smaller size of SDC's programs may act in its advantage as it is less likely to elicit political resistance. Additionally, the lower funding levels allow SDC to carefully design and test activities without spending pressures.

That set-up permits SDC to use different intervention strategies, depending on context and opportunities. In Bosnia and Herzegovina, for example, it occupies a niche focusing on support to the Prosecutor Offices. In Kosovo, it supports the functioning of Notary offices. In Tajikistan, its justice engagement has grown out of its efforts to eliminate gender-based violence and now center on legal aid services. In West Africa, again, its justice engagement is part of broader rural development interventions and is treated as a cross-cutting theme with a focus on conflict resolution and customary justice mechanisms. When supporting high-level and politicized reform processes, such as in Constitutional reform, SDC is likely to do so in collaboration with multilateral actors.

Challenges Ahead

Against the backdrop of these important strengths (and weaknesses that are being addressed institutionally), new challenges will likely shape SDC's justice engagement and that of other donors in the future.

SDC is not immune to the growing public skepticism about the lasting impact of development cooperation. While the adoption of the Agenda 2030 has undoubtedly been a major milestone globally, public opinions about development at the national levels have overall become less supportive. Alongside that skepticism, domestic policy agendas tend to increasingly influence development agencies. Agencies may more and more be asked to align their programs in accordance with priorities outside their core mandate, such as counter-terrorism, security, migration, and anti-trafficking, at times to an extent that bends the definition of what is commonly agreed as Official Development Assistance. (The definition of ODA, can be found at:

http://www.oecd.org/dac/stats/officialdevelopmentassistancedef initionandcoverage.htm

With such influence growing, there is a risk that development agencies and donors no longer have the ability to look at development challenges in a holistic and context-oriented manner, and instead, risk being asked to shape their programs to fit domestic priorities. In the justice sector, that may manifest itself in support to single justice issues (for example, setting up a separate courts system that is tasked to exclusively deal with terrorism cases; initiatives related to migration management; or hurried legislative reforms) that reflect domestic policy priorities by donor governments, but risk circumventing development strategies defined by host countries.

These approaches further risk reinforcing simplistic views that there are quick fixes to complex, transnational challenges. If justice programs are influenced in this manner, there is a risk of falling back into the old mistakes of replicating and designing programs in a top-down manner, but far from local realities. The space for decision-making given to development agencies will, in the future, thus be decisive about whether justice support programs use approaches that are adapted to the context within which it operates and ultimately benefit the people in partner countries.

Bolivia – Illustrating SDC's Access to Justice Support

Context

In Bolivia, the justice system has been working on resolving long-standing and structural issues. In the last 20 years, state-led reforms have been made aimed at restructuring the Judicial Branch, adapting the body of rules regulating organic laws, rewriting the State Political Constitution (2009), and at updating civil and criminal codes and others in the process of gradually transitioning to a public hearings system.

These reforms have had their shortcomings, mainly to do with a lack of established strategic alliances with the justice administration institutions and civil society, as well as insufficient budget allocated to the reform process. No real solutions have been installed to combat corruption, curb delays in bringing cases to trial, or ensure independence of the justice system, which are all critical issues to be solved as regards justice in the constitutional reform. In brief, reforms are seen through a highly technical-regulatory lens and little attention is being paid to their implementation, which limits the impact they are expected to have on citizens.

The contents of the new constitution are highly protectionist, recognizing that Bolivia is a state that promotes a culture of peace, and offers guarantees of due process including access to a justice system that is pluralistic, timely, free and transparent, and acts without undue delays. In order to avoid the highest-ranking judges being selected on the basis of their party affiliations in Congress, they are, instead, elected by popular vote, which in turn gives rise to a whole new set of problems; all too often judges prefer the political leanings of the electorate rather than applying the law.

Despite these long-standing reform efforts, the main structural problems persist: limited access to justice; too many trials being delayed; overcrowded prisons (exceeding the detention capacity by 300%); excessive use of pre-trial detention (70% of all detainees are held awaiting trial); judicial bias; insufficient budget allocated to the justice sector. These are further compounded by the widespread punitive culture in Bolivian society and people's overall lack of confidence in the justice system.

Another key issue is that the courts in the urban and metropolitan areas are unable to cope with the workload, as migration from rural areas to the country's three main cities (home to over 65% of the country's population) has caused the courts to collapse, making it even more difficult for people to access the system, especially those who are poor and vulnerable due to their economic and ethnic profile.

Elements of the Project Design for Greater Access to Justice

The foundations of SDC's ongoing Access to Justice (AJ) project have initially been laid with the 'Justice and Citizenship' programme (2005–2009), whose scope covered indigenous rights, the fight against corruption, and promoting dialogue and negotiating skills. Following, SDC's work concentrated on supporting the government's eradication of slavery and semi-slavery of indigenous groups, and was also complemented with the Citizenship Culture Programme (CCP), geared to empowering citizens through civil society at the municipal level (2009–2012).

The previous programs, which focussed on people exercising and protecting their rights, enabled SDC in Bolivia to design the AJ project (2013–2017) taking into account the previous experience. The aim of the AJ program was to identify an area that had real potential to improve people's access to effective justice. SDC chose to focus on 'conciliation', a form of alternative dispute resolution, as a mechanism for solving conflicts, along with a shift in the institutional and society paradigm to privilege a culture of peace over the current preference for filing lawsuits to solve a problem. This entailed the AJ project taking a different approach, and perhaps more importantly, taking on the challenge of committing to alternative ways of seeking justice that, in addition, require a good dose of political will to be implemented.

Efforts, therefore, have been focussed on advocating for a public policy on access to justice, especially for the most vulnerable groups (with emphasis on women, adolescents, and detainees). The AJ project contemplated three courses of action: Conciliation in the courts, strengthening the Public Defence Service, and implementing strategic actions to position and/or boost the public agenda of reforms for greater access to justice. The strategy was to do direct advocacy work at a national level by supporting conciliation proceedings before going to trial (civil cases). Simultaneously, the Ministry of Justice was supported to provide legal advice and out-of-court conciliation services. The work done by the latter has made significant progress. Working with civil society, Foundations and/or private Conciliation Centers, a large number of cases requested directly by the public are dealt with to facilitate solutions to civil disputes (e.g. debt-recovery) and family disputes (e.g. child maintenance and inheritances), reducing overall the number of hearings dealt with in court and saving the state resources.

Now, as the project gets ready to exit, several significant results have been identified. Among the most outstanding, the project contributed "… essentially to the implementation of alternative dispute resolution mechanisms; boosting the institutional capacities of the judicial branch; collaborating effectively to expand the range of services to facilitate access to justice, which has a direct link to enforcing rights, constitutional guarantees and mechanisms to balance the use of the court system; the effective involvement of civil society organizations in implementing public policy ... and supplied a model for legal services that has had good results and for which there is a growing demand." Overall, more than 70,000 persons benefited from increased access to justice.

The areas given priority by the AJ project were worked on from different angles with the corresponding counterparts. For the purpose of this chapter, we will concentrate on the experience of conciliation in the courtroom or courts.

The Challenges, Their Scope and the Manner in Which They Were Dealt

The project encountered a myriad of challenges, both at the level of reforms and their political and institutional implications, and because it sought to change the paradigm that justice was reserved for a privileged few and not trusted by most. Therefore, the first task was to understand as much as possible, the changes that were happening in the country, especially those being wrought in the justice sector and their political implications. The second task was to understand the needs of the users of the justice system and of the justice operators, by reflecting on the possible positive and negative impacts on them.

Therefore, beyond the painstaking work on the technical aspects, the AJ project prioritized the political and contextual elements that might affect the results planned for and agreed on with the project counterparts. This meant spending a considerable amount of time on building relations of trust with public employees and authorities, maintaining political dialogue with key actors, rolling out mitigation actions to handle conflict sensitively, providing technical support and generating evidence (data) for authorities to analyze and make evidence-based decisions, ensuring ownership, and building public-private networks. This was all crucial for advocacy work at the policy level and ensuring that priority groups have effective access to justice.

We faced resistance at the institutional level to incorporating the concept of conciliation into the court system. The judges would not acknowledge the conciliators; the figure of the judge as having the power to make the rulings was threatened by the appearance of a new way of resolving cases (conciliation), where the claimant (the main protagonist in conciliation processes) becomes a user of the service provided by a facilitator/conciliator and the solution is reached by both sides negotiating a win-win situation. Therefore, training judges and involving high court judges in visits to regional projects on conciliation (enabling learning across countries in the region) were essential to gaining their support and achieving progress.

Another key factor was 'process management'. It is well known that there is always resistance to change; however, this resistance can sometimes be overwhelming and may even sound the death knell for the change desired. Therefore, a Strategic Committee was formed with counterpart institutions to introduce conciliation to the high court judges. However, this did not work because of a lack of common understandings and goals, and due to complex infighting and power relations.

In order to solve the situation, a follow-up mechanism was rolled out, tasked to oversee the implementation of the conciliation. This follow-up mechanism included a group of representatives of key actors in the process: conciliators, judges, presidents of courts, high court judges, and SDC. These met regularly and supported by experts in conflict management, made decisions on how to solve problems as they arose, which slowly but surely led to results. In order for all of this to be successful, the information generated by the judicial officers, their commitment, and even more importantly, clear roles and responsibilities assigned to each actor were essential. The SDC was and is accompanying the process, providing financial and technical support when necessary, while being clear that it is the responsibility of the government to implement the conciliation mechanism. Currently, the judicial branch contributes 70% of funding to conciliation services while the SDC contributes the remaining 30%.

Lessons Learned to this Point

What stands out as relevant is a deep understanding of the technical and political dimensions of the process for objectives to be defined as coherent and achievable. Therefore, understanding the local context is crucial. The combination of context knowledge, dialogue, and political advocacy, especially with government entities at the national level, is key to making progress. The political, social, and cultural context of the country, and also of the region, has an impact on what actions donor support should take, and sufficient flexibility and ability to adapt to different contexts and political and institutional cycles is essential.

Understanding these processes needs to be done alongside the planning of long-term support as opposed to unrealistic short-term interventions. The conciliation project is part of a 12-year long support by SDC and will continue. It takes time and continuity for changes to be effective, as each preceding change becomes a building block for project actors, including civil society and aid agencies that work on the same issues. Processes need to be supported in a cyclical manner, meaning that it is important to advance, check the results, and consolidate achievements; it is also necessary to innovate and move forward until all elements have been taken on board, in particular ownership by national actors, which will ensure sustainability.

Building alliances and interacting with the government, civil society organizations, donors, and development partners are more likely to yield efficient results. Decision-making processes are influenced by many different factors, and so each entity needs to be consulted and their strengths used rather than creating a closed circle of actors that make all the decisions. As regards reforms, especially judicial reforms, raising public awareness is key to achieving results. The next phase of the AJ project, currently being drafted, will focus on consolidating conciliation to resolve family and civil disputes, and to include disputes between citizens and local governments, criminal offences, and minor infractions.

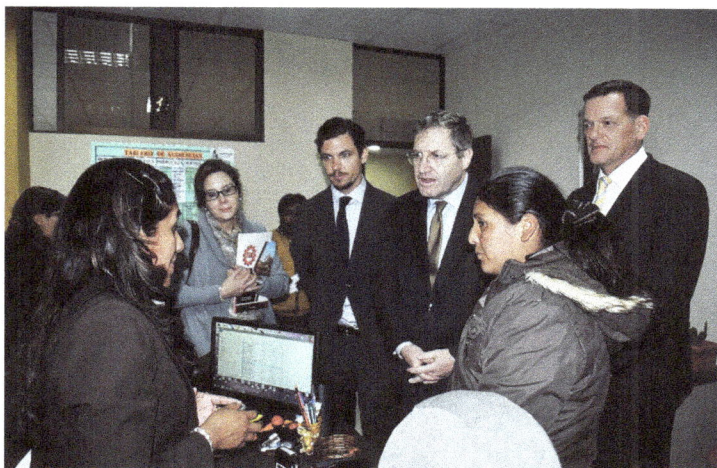
Swiss mission field visit to Courts of Justice, Bolivia 2018.

Conciliation campaign in native language, Bolivia.

Chapter 9
One Rule of Law Project in Post-Soviet Russia
Attorney Albert E. Scherr

I.   Introduction

Often ignored in an appreciation of a rule-of-law project, is the matter of context – the cultural context within which the project occurs. And in particular, the legal culture. This chapter focuses on two different sources for measuring the culture within which our project occurred between 1999 and 2004 in Vologda, Russia. That period was a time of particularly great transition in Russia from the Soviet era to the non-Soviet era. Such as it was, the Soviet era was one of cultural stability. For example, people who wanted to be lawyers knew what to expect and citizens knew what to expect from the legal system.

This chapter examines the culture in a provincial capital outside of the Moscow St. Petersburg axis. It uses two sources – our rule-of-law project and oral history of that time in Russia – to assess the context within which the project operated and to offer some interesting comparisons.

Svetlana Alexievich, the Nobel Prize winning author, has written compellingly of the Soviet people's transition to a post-Soviet era in her most recent book, *Secondhand Time: The Last of the Soviets*. In a unique reporting style that combines journalism and oral history, she documents the voices of former Soviet citizens as they make the transition to a new world of unpredictable dimensions.

Our rule of law project occurred primarily during the first ten years of this transition. Shortly after the end of our project, Vladimir Putin began to consolidate his power more assertively. Through their own words then, those in Alexievich's account capture well the intellectual, psychological, and financial turmoil of those transitional years. They provide a rich context for appreciating the efforts, successful and less so, of our 1999-2004 project.

It was a time of transition to the unknown. Hopes were high for some; money and capitalism meant more for some than it ever had; and both nostalgia and hatred for the Soviet era was common. Two in *Secondhand Time* spoke eloquently and directly about the transition:

> – Yeltsin's nineties ... how do we remember them? They were a happy time ... a crazy decade ...terrifying years ... the age of fantastical democracy ... the fatal nineties ... hands down, a golden age ... the age of self-denunciation ... mean and hard times ... a bright dawn ... aggressive ... turbulent ... That was my time ... It wasn't for me.
> – We pissed away the nineties! We're not going to have an opportunity like that again, at least not any time soon. Everything started out so well in '91! I'll never forget the faces of the people I stood with in front of the White House [the Russian government building at the center of a failed coup against Boris Yeltsin]. We were triumphant, we were powerful. We wanted to live. We were intoxicated by freedom. But now ... now I see it all in a different light ... We were so naïve, it's disgusting! Brave, honest, and naïve. We believed that salami was spontaneously generated by freedom. We too are to blame for everything that happened afterward ... Of course, Yeltsin is also responsible, but so are we. [1]

The post-Soviet era began with the sort of soaring hopes expressed above. And, at least by the accounts of many in the book, the result, and perhaps value of that 'freedom', quickly became the pursuit of money in a new, wildly capitalistic, economic world. The resulting dynamic of disappointed hopes and new money is apparent throughout *Secondhand Time.* It

---

[1] Svetlana Alexievich, *Secondhand Time: The Last of The Soviets,* (translated by Bela Shayevich), p. 287, Random House, New York, 2016

operates as the foundational context through which all else flowed:

> When I was young, I liked to toy with my fate, to tempt it. Not anymore; I've had enough. My daughter is growing up, I need to think of her future. And that means money! I want to make it myself. I don't want to ask anyone else for it, or to take it from anyone. I have no desire for that! I quit the newspaper and went to work for an advertising agency, the pay is better. It's good money. People are interested in the beautiful life, that's the most important thing happening today. It's what's on everyone's mind.[2]

Several recurrent and overlapping themes in particular resonate in the context of our rule-of-law project. Whether one's formative years – loosely ten to twenty-five years old – were during the Soviet era or during the post-Soviet transition, appears as a somewhat reliable predictor of attitudes about money, politics, and the past and future, at least for Alexievich's people:

> My sons were little boys back then [at the time of the end of the Soviet era], they've grown up since. One of them is even married. Several times, I tried … I want to tell them about 1991 … 1993 … but they're not interested. Their eyes would glaze over. The only question they have for me is, "Papa, why didn't you get rich in the nineties, back when it was so easy?" As though the only people who didn't get rich were the armless and dumb. Your cretin ancestors … kitchen impotents … We were too busy running around to protests. Sniffing the air of freedom while the smart ones divvied up the oil and gas …[3]

And:

> There's one thing I know for sure: Capitalism is not what my parents ordered. No two ways about it. It's what I

[2] *Id.,* at 348–49.
[3] *Id.*, at 289–90.

ordered, it's made for people like me, who didn't want to stay in the cage. The young and the strong. For us, capitalism was exciting ... adventures in enterprise, risk ... It's not just about money. The mighty dollar! Now I'll reveal my secret: For me, capitalism, I mean modern capitalism, not Dreiser, is more interesting to read about than the gulag or Soviet shortages. The informants. Oh! Oh! Gosh, I've trod on the sacred. I wouldn't dare breathe a word of this to my parents. My lips are sealed. How could I! My father remains a Soviet romantic.[4]

What to make of the Soviet past mattered notably to many of those in *Secondhand Time*, just as it seemed to matter in Vologda, at least amongst those we encountered. Some of Alexievich's people spoke of disdain and some of nostalgia for that time:

[In the Soviet era,] [w]e read, we went through tons of books. We talked. We thought we were coming up with new ideas. We dreamt of revolution, but we were scared we'd never live to see it. In reality, we were completely sheltered, we didn't know a thing about what was actually going on in the world. We were like houseplants. We made everything up, and as it later turned out, everything we thought we knew was nothing but figments of our imaginations: The West. Capitalism. The Russian people. We lived in a world of mirages. The Russia of our books and kitchens never existed. It was all in our heads.[5]

By contrast:

What did I feel? Did I believe in the Party? To tell you the truth, I did. And I still do. Come what may, I will never throw out my Party membership card. Did I believe in communism? I'll be honest with you, I'm not going to lie: I believe in the possibility of life being governed fairly. And today ... as I've already told you ... I still believe in that.

---

[4] *Id.*, at 339.

[5] *Id.*, at p. 19.

I'm sick of hearing how bad life was under socialism. I'm proud of the Soviet era! It wasn't 'the good life', but it was regular life. We had love and friendship ... dresses and shoes ... People hungrily listened to writers and actors, which they don't do anymore.[6]

Finally, the different worlds of St. Petersburg/Moscow and everywhere else in the post-Soviet world is tangible throughout *Secondhand Time*, and throughout every day of ours as we traveled to Vologda through St. Petersburg and Moscow.

[To Alexievich:] You're on the right track, leaving Moscow. You could say that you've come to the real Russia. Walking around Moscow, you might get the impression that we're a European country: the luxury cars, the restaurants ... those golden cupolas gleaming ... Moscow is the capital of some other nation, not the country beyond the ring road. A tourist paradise. Don't believe Moscow ...[7]

And:

Capitalism isn't taking root here. The spirit of capitalism is foreign to us. It never made it out of Moscow. We don't have the proper climate for it in the rest of the country. And we're not the right people.[8]

That is not to say that these are rigidly defined themes either in Alexievich's accounts or in our experience. The rich, layered complexity of the worlds her people recount is not easily captured in tidy thematic boxes. Here post-Soviet people are people trying to understand and grasp for themselves, the meaning of the profound transition in which they have found themselves with little prior notice. And, our rule of law project confronted much the same transitional complexity, but by

---

[6] *Id.*, at 53.

[7] *Id.*, at 42. The ring road is the major road that encircles Moscow.

[8] *Id.*, at 293.

choice and with the perspective of outsiders amidst people in an unfamiliar world.

II. The Project

We received U.S. State Department funding for a rule of law project in northern Russia from 1999–2004. The grant had three parties: The University of New Hampshire (UNH), Franklin Pierce Law Center (FPLC) (now University of New Hampshire School of Law (UNH Law)), and Vologda State Pedagogical University (VSPU), in particular the law faculty at VSPU. The co-directors from the U.S. side were a tenured UNH historian of Russia, who was fluent in Russia and a tenured law professor at FPLC. That combination provided the project with a deep background in Russian history, culture and institutions, and in legal education. Originally, the project had a three-year funding cycle. It received two one-year, no-cost extensions.

Vologda is a provincial capital of around 300,000 people in northern Russia, about halfway between Moscow and Archangelsk. The Vologda Oblast, as a whole, has about 1.2 million residents. The principal economic drivers in Vologda and the region are ferrous metallurgy, power engineering, and timber, as well as it being a substantial transportation hub. The region is also known for its 'Vologda butter' and its lace-making.

VSPU was founded in 1918 and is formally accredited by the Ministry of Education and Science of the Russian Federation. At the time of the project, it had about 3,500 students in the university as a whole. The law school itself, however, was much younger, founded in the late Soviet era.

III. The Vision – Pedagogy as a Mechanism for a Change in the Rule of Law Culture

The grant sought to further the growth of the rule of law in Russia. Furtherance of that goal had already taken many forms since the end of the Soviet era. Scholars, government officials, and others counseled lawmakers and governmental executives, on everything from constitutional principles to the drafting of new laws. Lawyers, law professors, and others advised legislators and administrators on the development of new legal processes and structures. Judges and others exchanged ideas and practices with their counterparts on the bench, about decision-making and doctrine.

Changing legal principles, processes, and institutions in the furtherance of the rule of law is important and difficult. Those changes are the front-end of a much longer-term process of changing the legal culture in the broadest sense. A legal culture in which lawyers, judges, and citizens trust the system to operate well and effectively is the essence of the term 'rule of law'. The premise underlying the activities of this grant took the challenge of changing legal principles, processes, and institutions one step further, by focusing on a different aspect of cultural change – legal pedagogy. The focus on pedagogical practices presumed that the existence of a rule of law society – a civil society – depended not only on the development of principles, processes, and institutions, but also on the development of a rule of law *culture*. And, a rule-of-law culture is best developed using the tools of education, writ large.

To press the point a bit, legal culture and cultural attitudes about law, influence human behavior in the realm of law at least as much as the presence of legal principles, processes, and institutions do. In part, of course, culture and its attitudes owe their existence to the presence of principles, processes, and institutions. An aggrieved citizen will not have the instinct to use the legal system to address her complaint without the existence of a viable system, i.e., a culture of seeking redress in a system that produces reliable results.

Yet, the existence of a viable legal system – one based on sound principles, processes, and institutions – is not enough. Unless the aggrieved citizen trusts her instinct to use the system to address her complaint, a rule of law society does not exist. And, unless lawyers within the system – particularly a changing legal system – trust the principles, processes, and institutions enough to take advantage of it, a rule-of-law society/culture does not exist.

The issue of legal culture and cultural attitudes towards law was particularly significant in post-Soviet Russia. The rule-of-law literature and conversations with judges and lawyers in Russia, confirmed that a legal system based on principles, processes, and institutions existed even in the Soviet era, at least in theory. But, the perception that it was a functioning system – that one could trust in the instinct to use it – did not exist. One's relationship – financial, familial, or otherwise – with the local party boss still determined more as to the outcome of one's grievance than did the legal system. If not always actually true, this appeared to be the general perception of most in Soviet Russia.

> In Soviet Russia, then, the existence of the principles, processes, and institutions did not give rise to a functioning system automatically. Put simply, the common assumption – "if you build it, they will come" – was false. The result in post-Soviet Russia – at least as revealed anecdotally in conversations with practicing lawyers seeking clients – was that an aggrieved citizen remains unlikely to seek out legal assistance to address the complaint. And, this was the case even with a better functioning rule-of-law system.[9]

Change in the legal culture and cultural attitudes about law become important in this context. Such change would increase the likelihood that changes in legal principles, processes, and institutions will endure beyond the current investment of time, energy, and money. The complex and diffuse origins of cultural attitudes towards law, however, make such change difficult and slow. Likely, such change develops over several generations, if ever.

The activities of the grant constituted an effort to use a focus on legal pedagogy to begin to effectuate a change in the cultural attitudes of law professors and future lawyers towards law. If one teaches law in a participatory, active, and engaged environment, students perceive their role as lawyers differently and more positively. If one teaches with role-playing exercises

---

[9] For example, interestingly, albeit anecdotally, law students in Vologda, when questioned about what they would do if they were in a car accident or the victim of a crime, most often answered that they would rely on the informal, process-free, pseudo-black-market justice system to resolve the matter rather than use the formal justice system.

and simulations, future lawyers will, by habit and instinct, become more active participants in the legal system. If one creates a learning environment in which law students are respected and valued for their challenges to a teacher's authority, they become more effective advocates for their future clients' rights.

We also came to the project with substantial concerns about the risk of being perceived as legal imperialists. It was, and is, a risk that travels with any rule-of-law project. Intended or otherwise, rule-of-law projects are quite easily perceived as conveying a message of: "We know the right way to do things and we will now tell you the best way to do it." We perceived that risk to be particularly acute in a post-Soviet Russia, in which many of the more senior positions in the local and regional legal systems outside the Moscow/St. Petersburg axis were still filled with holdovers from the Soviet era. And, this was likely true of most of the practicing lawyers who had been trained in the old Soviet system.

In that vein, a focus on legal pedagogy as a vector for change in the legal culture of post-Soviet Russia, was more nuanced and less top-down. We wanted to expose law professors to alternatives for engaging students, and even more fundamentally, at least considering the engagement of students as of value. We aspired to provide them with an expanded set of pedagogical options rather than a list of rules to follow. Our fundamental belief was that evolution of techniques in legal education held great promise for sustainable cultural change in rule of law attitudes.

IV. Implementation of the Vision

Broadly, the framework for project implementation centered on visits of various lengths on the part of UNH/UNH Law and VSPU faculty. Over the grant's five years, ten VSPU faculty, including the Dean of the law school, visited UNH and UNH Law. Two of them spent almost a full academic year at UNH/UNH Law and four more spent a full academic semester there. The remainder spent anywhere from one to four weeks on campus in New Hampshire.

A total of five UNH/UNH Law senior faculty, two graduate students, and one evaluator made visits to VSPU, ranging from one to three weeks during the grant's five years. Several of the senior faculty members made a number of trips to Vologda. In addition, three UNH/UNH Law faculty visited the law school in Saint Petersburg to engage in discussions with a number of faculty there about Russian and U.S. legal education.

More specifically, the VSPU faculty engaged in a wide range of activities designed to further the pedagogical focus of the project's vision. For example:

- they observed classroom instruction at UNH and UNH Law to consider different pedagogical approaches;
- they attended classes regularly at UNH Law and UNH whose content contributed to their research and teaching specialization;
- they consulted with UNH and UNH Law professors about course content, pedagogical methods, judicial and legal practices in the U.S. and research interests;
- they lectured in UNH Law and UNH courses (in one case, team-taught a full course);
- they pursued independent research in FPLC and UNH libraries to gather materials for their teaching in Vologda and their research projects;
- they learned how to use information technologies and databases to access materials for their research and teaching;
- they learned how to use PowerPoint and other technology tools for teaching;
- visited law offices, courts, and government agencies in New Hampshire and Maine;
- they made public presentations in New Hampshire and Maine about Russian law and its legal system;
- they traveled to Washington to meet with members of the NH Congressional delegation, observe the Supreme Court in session, and tour the Capitol; and
- they attended conferences of the American Association for the Advancement of Slavic Studies.

The UNH/UNH Law faculty also engaged in a wide range of activities. For example:

- they provided mini-courses or lectures on subjects in U.S. law requested by Vologda instructors (international human rights law, consumer protection law, criminal procedure in the jury system, DNA/scientific evidence in criminal cases, environmental law, media role during election campaigns, terror, and civil liberties);
- they assisted in the establishment and development of the legal clinic in Vologda (the only legal clinic in the Vologda region);
- they attended a national conference in St. Petersburg in year two on the development of legal clinics, in the company of the grant participant designated to establish and direct the Vologda legal clinic;
- they observed classroom instruction and end-of-the-year student exams and thesis presentations;
- they met with groups of students to discuss their attitudes toward the rule of law;
- they ran workshops on pedagogical methods;
- they made several public presentations to local government officials; and
- they purchased instructional technology and library books for the law school.

Perhaps most productively, the participating faculty of UNH Law, UNH, and VSPU all produced articles for a volume about legal pedagogy in Russian law schools. The volume was published by a Vologda printer and circulated to all the law schools in Russia. It included an introduction written by a justice on the Constitutional Court of the Russian Federation, who previously had been a law professor at the law school in St. Petersburg.

What remains most vivid about these activities are the personal encounters with students, young faculty, and senior faculty and administration. On innumerable occasions, I met with individual students as well as groups. Invariably, their thirst was less for substantive knowledge and more along the lines of 'how to be a lawyer'. They quickly understood that the lawyer models in Soviet Russia were different than those which we offered up through our teaching and our simulations.

For example, each time I visited VSPU, I conducted a simulated jury trial with students playing the role of witnesses and jurors as my colleagues and I played the role of lawyers. In the debriefing following the simulation, students were endlessly curious about both the details and the broad concepts. Some were focused on how one made the many in-trial litigation decisions; while others were focused on why you would ever want a jury that might contain 'peasants' as opposed to a trial before an 'expert' judge. Always, questions about substance and procedure took a back seat to questions about, loosely, psychology and strategy [10] – thinking and talking about behaving like a lawyer and what the many models of lawyering looked like.

Conversations and teaching demonstrations with young faculty were similarly vibrant and engaging. Again, the focus was less on the substantive and procedural content of what we were discussing.[11] They were much more riveted on the simple decision to actively engage students in the classroom; to encourage them to challenge the professor or each other; or to cede control of the classroom in some measure to the students.

These moments occurred, year after year, during the project, and seemed to be a reflection of a feeling of being unshackled on the part of participating students and faculty, at least from our perspective. In private conversations with younger faculty, they frequently complained about the leveling or narrowing effect of having to meet the curricular demands imposed by the Ministry of Education nationwide. They also felt pressure from the VSPU administration and older 'Soviet' faculty to toe the line.

* * * * * * * *

These experiences with students and younger faculty were very much in line with the results of a survey we conducted of

---

[11] if only because German law was the jurisdiction outside Russia to whom they looked for substance and procedure in the first instance

144

VSPU law students in the last year of the project, 2004. The survey was designed to begin to discern what the nascent legal culture of those coming of age in the post-Soviet era looked like. For example:

- Why did they choose to study law?
- What did they expect to do with their law degree?
- What do they think of lawyers and the place of law in society?

We wanted to get some sense of what kind of nascent legal culture might exist amongst those who had just decided to go to law school, ten years into the post-Soviet period of transition.

We surveyed a total of 73 students. 61% of those surveyed were female and 39% male. 46% were in their first year, 32% in their second year, and 21% in their third year. 70% of the group was born in the Vologda region. Their average age was 19.9 years old, and the age at which they decided to study law averaged 15.7 years old. About 20% 0f the group believed they were fluent enough in a foreign language to read its legal materials.

Their expectations upon completing their study of law seemed unsurprising and quite practical.

- Pursue a job as a lawyer – 66.7%
- Pursue a job in a government office of some kind – 31.9%
- Pursue another degree in law – 16.7%
- Pursue a job in a business company – 16.7%
- Pursue a job teaching law – 1.4%
- Pursue another degree in an area other than law – 13.6%
- Pursue a job in a bank – 12.5%

Remember that this group, on average, was born around 1985. They were about eight years old when the Soviet Union fell, and they came of age in the most chaotic part of a societal transition to an unknown post-Soviet future – the remainder of the 1990s. As the century turned, many were reaching their decision to study law. We asked them what were their reasons for going to law school.[12]

The themes we saw in Alexievich's *Secondhand Time* appear differently here. In terms of their teenaged aspirations, this group was not primarily concerned about how much money they could make, about their self-interest, or about social/political status. Rather, the reasons for attending law school with which they most strongly agreed involved: (1) the importance of a strong legal system; (2) helping family, friends, injured people, and those who can't help themselves.[13] Notably less frequent reasons for attending law school included: (1) family influences; (2) gaining political power; (3) modeling Putin's background; and (4) the ease of studying law.[14] As a group, they were in agreement or more neutral as to: (1) making or overcoming obstacles to making money; (2) gaining influence; and (3) gaining respect.[15]

At the least then, on the threshold of the study of law, this rural group of teenagers seemed to reflect optimism and idealism – perhaps typical attitudes for aspirational teenagers, but nonetheless noteworthy in a rural capital outside of the Moscow/St. Petersburg axis during a time of dramatic social/psychological, economic, and political change.

More broadly, when asked more directly about their feelings as to a number of propositions related to a legal culture in Russia, [16] they responded even more interestingly. The group's optimism and idealism about the role of law and lawyers shines through even more strongly in these results. The importance (1) of the Russian Constitution (an aspirational document even in Soviet times); (2) of a strong legal system

---

[12] See Appendix for full results for Question # 1.

[13] Their agreement with these reasons ranges from 1.5 – the midpoint between 'strongly agree' and 'agree' to 1.94 – almost squarely on 'agree'.

[14] Their neutrality as to or disagreement with these reasons ranged from 3.01 – squarely on 'neutral' – and

[15] Their agreement with or neutrality as to these reasons ranged from 2.44 – close to the midpoint between agreement and neutrality to 2.99 – essentially, squarely on neutrality.

[16] See Appendix for full results for Question # 2.

that both protected individuals and was accessible to everyone; and (3) of lawyers that helped the injured, worked to change bad laws, and used their power to help others, predominated. Those ideas were the only propositions receiving average scores between 'agree' and 'strongly agree'. Even in the closer-to-agree section[17] of the 'agree' to 'neutral', agreement with similar propositions again predominated.

Interestingly, in the neutral-to-disagree section, the group moderates the importance of lawyers in comparison to other professions. They tend to disagree with the idea that lawyers are more respected than artists, scholars, doctors, scientists, and business people. It seems to represent a measure of practicality in their appreciation of the lawyers, i.e., they perform an important role but, as a profession, are no better than others.

More notably, the group diminishes the importance of the legal system as one designed to protect government and commercial interests, as well as, more generally, the interests of those with power. Laid against what Alexievich's people describe as the cynicism of the late Soviet and early post-Soviet eras, these attitudes about the legal system express either a healthy dose of naiveté; an idealism and optimism not substantially reduced by the first twenty years of their life; or both. And, once again, notably absent in those propositions with which they most agreed, were those related to the desire to make money and the earning power of lawyers – a distinct contrast with the raging capitalism of the post-Soviet transition frequently noted by the voices in *Secondhand Time.*

* * * * * * * *

Much more nuanced and subtle conclusions might be drawn from this collection of data. But what stands in starkest contrast to the above results, is the much darker attitudes of the older professors and the administration at VSPU – those who came to maturity in the Soviet era. As a group, they wanted nothing to do with our project other than what money and free trips to the United States they could acquire from the project. With one exception, the more senior professors either ignored

---

[17] *i.e.,* below a 2.5 average

us or spoke ill of us, both behind our backs and to our faces. And, the one exception to this cold reception had been fired by the end of the project, apparently because of his leadership role in the project.

The administration of the law faculty at VSPU was even more problematic. The Dean was an ex-Soviet bureaucrat who examined every aspect of the project closely. His primary interest was to arrange for students to be part of the exchange with UNH and UNH Law. In particular, he wanted students to travel to the U.S. as part of the exchange – a practice prohibited by the terms of our grant authorization. This prohibition was of little consequence to him and we, an ABA/CEELI officer from Moscow, and a State Department consular official, all were the subject of one or more screaming, table-pounding tirades on the part of the Dean.

Beyond that behavior, and likely as a consequence of his frustration with the travel prohibition for students, he made the professional lives of his VSPU colleagues who participated in the grant quite difficult. He criticized them publicly and isolated them from more senior, Soviet-era faculty. He fired the co-director of the project for being absent for two weeks of teaching, during a time when the co-director was engaged in grant activities of which he had informed the administration. Stunningly, a judge who reviewed the firing made a finding that the grant did not actually exist, though that very judge had visited New Hampshire as a part of an ABA/CEELI project and was fully aware of the State Department rule of law project.

Professor Frierson, the UNH co-director of the project has described his behavior as "the embodiment of *proviso*, that is, arbitrary and capricious behavior that is the antithesis of the rule of law."[18] In more depth, Professor Frierson has used the landmark study by Konstantin Simis, *USSR: The Corrupt Society*[19], as a reference point for the Dean's behavior.

---

[18] A. Scherr & C. Frierson, ***A Rule-of-Law Project Meets 'Arbitrary & Capricious' Obstacles in Vologda, Russia***, 44 N.H. Bar Journal 19–24 (2003)

[19] Konstantin Simis, *USSR: The Corrupt Society: The Secret World of Soviet Capitalism,* Simon & Schuster, *1982.*

As a former lawyer in the Soviet judicial system in Moscow, Simis gathered evidence of local abuses of power by officials who were in a position to control both their subordinates and ordinary citizens through their hold over employment, housing, and resources. Simis dubbed these officials the 'District Mafia' because of their similarity to neighborhood dons, who simultaneously were able to provide benefits outside the law and to control and extort outside the law.[20] And, she used William Tubman's biography of Nikita Khrushchev[21] as an additional reference point for the Dean's behavior.

His modus operandi was a combination of hypersensitivity to perceived slights or condescension and pugnacious, rude, aggressive behaviors designed to preempt, unsettle, and ultimately disable those inside the Communist Party or in the foreign services of western powers (most notably the U.S.) in any negotiation, indeed, in any meeting.[22]

The difficulties with the Dean and his superiors led to a temporary suspension of the grant as we decided whether to spend the remaining grant funds in the midst of a difficult situation. Eventually, we resumed the relationship with an intensified focus on our individual relationships with students and the younger faculty, rather than VSPU as an institution.

In retrospect, our experience in Vologda was, in at least some regards, predictable in light of what Alexievich's people say. As a city outside the Moscow/St. Petersburg axis, change was likely coming at a different pace – deeply entrenched, old institutions, and those who run them, were perhaps changing more slowly, particularly when there is little pressure from anywhere to change, except from those who are effectively within one's control, i.e., students and younger faculty. In the short term then, the hope for immediate, more institutional change, was illusory.

Yet, we also found students that had an optimism and idealism about their reasons for wanting to be lawyers and their

---

[20] Scherr & Frierson, *A Rule-of-Law Project* ... p. 22

[21] William Taubman, *Khrushchev: The Man and His Era,* W.W. Norton, 2004.

[22] Scherr & Frierson, *A Rule-of-Law Project* ... p. 22–23.

view of the role of law in society. And, their commitment to learning about aggressive and proactive lawyering through participatory pedagogy was noteworthy. They represented a very small sample in one provincial region of a group of nascent professionals thinking about more than simply making money, in contrast to that which Alexievich's people hinted at as the primary focus of the non-Soviet 'younger generation'.

The younger faculty showed a similar excitement about the opportunities to try out new pedagogy; to start a legal clinic and to engage their students in class discussions. That many of them ended up leaving VSPU for other institutions or types of employment, is both unsettling and reveals a desire to seek a situation that suited that which they wanted, at least as articulated to us.

Rule-of-law projects in circumstances like ours are, at best, preliminary efforts at cultural change. One can change the rules of a legal system but, without a change in the legal culture, such changes are quite vulnerable. Endless debate surrounds the question of how best to effectuate such change in a legal culture. Do rule/law changes lead institutions, professionals to adapt and effectively change the culture over time, or does the injection of new and different voices bring about a change over time that makes institutional and rule/law change more likely?

Our project caught inklings of a great willingness for imbuing a legal system with new attitudes and perspectives, and so for progress towards a more profound legal-culture change. Those new attitudes and perspectives were not a result of our project; rather, they came to the fore as we opened the dialogue. Helping faculty and students nurture and support each other in their approaches, and over time, helping them grow into roles in the institutions themselves, was a sequence of rule of law projects for the future. One can only wonder where these 1999–2004 students and faculty are now and what they are doing.

* * * * * * * *

Chapter 10
Small Things Do Matter
Attorney William Meyer

A smile flashed across his face as he received his certificate. Though not the strongest student, his enthusiasm during the training was genuine. He loved being there.

Around him, scores of young folks smiled, waiting their turns in the sub-tropical heat. All knew that he was the 'minder', assigned by the military-controlled government to monitor the program. Tongues stayed in check, with excited conversations focused on the novelty of interactive teaching and role-playing exercises. Czech colleagues signaled that the building was closing, time to head for street food at the Takafuji.

Venues change, but challenges remain. Small person-to-person initiatives begun twenty-five years ago by volunteer lawyers have morphed into instruments of national policy. Academics and development professionals debate the efficacy of the entire law reform effort. Do long days spent mentoring young Burmese up-country lawyers move the rule of law needle?

In the sweltering heat, time for a beer.

* * * * * * * *

One dark evening in November 1989, television images stunned the world. For a small-town Iowa boy reared during the Cold War, the fall of the Berlin Wall was breathtaking. Now a trial lawyer in Colorado, my firm periodically provided each partner with a one-year, paid sabbatical. I wanted in on the action.

My opportunity came via the American Bar Association's fledgling Central and East European Law Initiative (CEELI). A self-funded trip to Washington, D.C. in July 1991 netted Jane and me a commitment for single roundtrip ticket to Bulgaria, plus a $200 per month stipend for three months, to prove that a lawyer from Boulder could provide meaningful assistance in that emerging democracy. Dubious about the prospects, careful ABA lawyers labeled me as merely a 'liaison', to enhance plausible deniability in the event that I created some embarrassment.

We landed in Bulgaria in early September 1991, a few days after the aborted coup in the then-existing Soviet Union. Our contact was a young Bulgarian law student, who met us in a broken-down Lada and ushered us to a shabby apartment in Sofia's Lenin Estates. Few officials – American or Bulgarian – knew or particularly cared that we arrived.

Instead of joining the ex-patriate community, our world became decidedly Bulgarian. With no budget, we slowly developed a volunteer network of local students and young lawyers eager to learn about Western systems. Their help allowed us to develop relationships with a variety of governmental, judicial, and Bar officials. For months, we avoided offering, and in fact refused to offer, advice to our new Bulgarian friends. The goal was to learn their system, their issues, and their concerns.

When the Socialists fell in late 1991, many of our Bulgarian contacts moved into the new government. Prior casual conversations turned into business meetings. With the support of dedicated ABA volunteers and staff, a lawyer from Colorado was able to provide technical assistance to the emerging leadership on a wide range of topics. We left Sofia a year after our arrival, feted on national television by Bulgarian and American officials, and delivered to the airport's VIP lounge by a Foreign Ministry limousine.

* * * * * * * *

Since 1992, I have been privileged to volunteer in a variety of capacities on rule of law projects across the globe. From Armenia to Ukraine, from Libya to Syria, from Cambodia to Kenya – this work has taken me to more than twenty countries. As a practicing attorney coming from outside the national and multi-national bureaucracies, and the professional development world, my lens remains 'client-centric'. What is best for the 'clients', the citizens of the affected country? From this perspective, some observations are in order.

By the mid-1990s, particularly after the fall of the Soviet Union, legal reform and assistance programs moved from the realm of volunteerism to become a significant component of government-sponsored development efforts. The professionalization of these programs added resources, but also created bureaucratic pressures to produce 'quantifiable results' to justify the increased outlays. At the same time, geopolitical forces began to intrude as nations began using law reform efforts as a component of their parochial foreign policies.

One manifestation of these trends was a shift toward larger-scale, institutional showcase projects, typically focused on providing senior judicial and governmental officials with advanced infrastructure and travel opportunities. The theory was that the quick and quantifiable advancements in the rule of law demanded by donor politicians were best obtained through a top-down strategy focused on institutions and buy-in from the upper echelons of the existing systems. This strategy had the collateral benefit of providing donors with opportunities to reward influential members of a country's political elite, enhancing the donor's political influence.

On one occasion, I was approached by a senior Bulgarian official, part of a 'study group' organized by a Western government and flown at great fanfare to various capitals to observe their counterparts in action. With his colleagues, the official had visited a number of places long off limits to Communist-Bloc functionaries. As the tours were coming to an end, he asked if they could 'borrow' one of my bright law student assistants to serve as a translator. The trips were wonderful, he explained, but no one thought to provide them with a translator capable of dealing with the arcane concepts relevant to this area of the law. Reluctant to complain to their hosts and potentially lose future travel opportunities, the study group, nonetheless, was curious to actually learn about some of the topics at hand.

The bureaucratization of rule of law efforts also led to the exultation of metrics, a quest to accurately measure the efficacy of a particular project in achieving the target goal. Required by those minding the purse strings, the pursuit of hard evidence of success produces various impacts. One is the insistence on pre-selected, measurable, and achievable project goals typically prepared by the donor. Tens of millions of dollars, euros and pounds have been spent developing project proposals with narrowly defined goals and intricate metrics to measure success. Projects may be selected based on their ability to produce a blip on some expensive metric prepared by the donor, rather than any ability to meet the practical needs of the recipient country.

Efforts to create assessment and measurement tools, while perhaps laudable, are inherently suspect. Several years ago, I participated in a focus group to review a new metric developed by a consulting firm under a seven-figure government contract. Nearly thirty experts were flown into Central Europe from various countries in the region to hear the presentation. Gathered in a darkened auditorium, our group was treated to a multi-media fanfare followed by a narrator enthusiastically describing the brilliant new creation. Suddenly, my foreign friends turned to the back of the room, gesturing at their headsets. In the booths behind, silent and bewildered translators threw up their hands. The producers had selected a variety of American football terms to describe the complex metric, baffling the European translators and English-speaking Europeans alike. Tone deafness of this sort too often arises when form is elevated over substance.

Perhaps more destructive, assessment fatigue has overtaken many parts of the world. Some local officials report being 'assessed' a dozen times or more, without a single substantive program ever being commenced. Slickly bound assessment reports sit in stacks in offices around the world, their recommendations unread and unrealized. Yet still the assessors come, seeking to develop a new baseline for yet another potential project.

At the same time, students and those at the lower rungs of the judiciary, Bar, and academia often are ignored. Such individuals had little clout and were viewed by some in the 'Old Guard' as potential threats. Few were able to produce the sort of rapid, visible results demanded by donor politicians. As a result, programs for street lawyers, trial judges, younger law professors, and students frequently received short shrift, in favor of higher profile initiatives potentially requiring less work and offering better optics.

* * * * * * * *

Debates about the meaning of 'the rule of law' rage throughout the legal community. While the definitional debate continues, after more than four decades of practicing law in the United States, one attribute of that concept stands out for me: A nation embraces the rule of law when its citizens voluntarily and customarily use the legal system to settle their disputes, and the results are accepted without undue rancor.

One central goal of legal reform and assistance programs should be to foster this type of trust throughout the general population. Yet in most fragile states and developing democracies, this trust is absent. A Balkan friend once quoted a regional aphorism: "The law is like a door in an open field – only a fool walks through it."

How can such attitudes be moderated? A silver bullet is unlikely. Far more likely is decades of trust-building, one citizen at a time. Positive interactions by citizens with the legal community in their daily lives, eventually, will create trust where none exists today. The front line of this battle is not some high court or ministry. Trust will be won by those on the front line: lawyers, prosecutors, and judges who deal with citizens on the mundane but (to average citizens) vitally important day-to-day matters that characterize all legal systems.

Too often, legal assistance programs ignore the men and women who must deal with the property disputes, employment claims, traffic offenses, and inheritance issues that typically bring ordinary folks into contact with the legal system. Throughout the developed and developing world alike, these lawyers, prosecutors, and judges do much to create or destroy the faith of the populace in that system. In well-functioning systems, these practitioners are trusted, and their words and actions enhance confidence in legal institutions. Yet in many instances, programs to develop their skills and expertise in emerging systems are underemphasized or absent.

To a large extent, these outcomes are a matter of choice, not chance. Years ago, a friend warned about the seductiveness of the 'easy contacts'. Senior judges, prosecutors, Bar leaders, and government officials often are relatively easy to access through well-developed channels, and eager to accept proffered programs that enhance their influence. Those further down the systemic food chain – who deal with ordinary citizens on a daily basis – may be harder to find, less sophisticated, and more concerned with daily affairs than enhancing the rule of law.

Yet it is these more anonymous individuals, manning the front lines of the legal system, who have major impacts on the development of the rule of law in a country. Citizens' trust in the legal system is fractured when they are confronted by corrupt or incompetent first-instance judges, politically manipulated prosecutors, or lawyers selling influence rather than acumen. Assistance programs focused on more prominent, easier-to-reach targets, seldom touch this critical bottom layer in a legal system.

* * * * * * * *

Sitting in the bed of a tiny Toyota pickup hurrying down the dusty thoroughfares of Mandalay, I admired at the swarms of heavily laden motorbikes positioned an arm's length away. Nearly a quarter century after squeezing into a rickety Lada to begin a life-changing journey in the Balkans, the scene had shifted to Southeast Asia where another nation struggled to escape decades of autocratic rule.

During the intervening years, I had been involved with legal assistance programs of many iterations. Some involved the high-level meetings with leaders such as Václav Havel or Bashar al-Assad. Other missions seemed almost clandestine, such as hitching a midnight ride through the snowy Caucasus in Karachay-Cherkessia with a Russian militia officer, speeding through the desert to Sirte with Palestinian colleagues near the end of the Libyan Revolution, or tramping in the dark through the Montenegrin no-man's land to meet with the newly independent regime in Podgorica. Most programs were more mundane.

After careening across oncoming traffic, we entered a small compound containing the open-air classroom where more than 100 waited under a lazy ceiling fan. Their story, and the story of how we came to be in Myanmar, illustrate the challenges and choices facing efforts to enhance the rule of law.

* * * * * * * *

In the distant past, Burmese considered law to be an elite profession. To enter, a student was required to obtain a post-graduate law degree from the Rangoon University, where courses were taught predominantly in English.

After a 1962 coup d'état and the establishment of a socialist state, student protests led to the revocation of the University's autonomy. A new, socialist-inspired legal curriculum was adopted, with only 100 to 150 students per year allowed into the program. The new regime also stacked the courts with retired members of the military, most lacking any formal legal training. This new system became an arm of military rule tasked to maintain political control.

New anti-government student demonstrations in the mid-1970s led the regime to close Burmese universities. When the universities reopened, the government introduced 'correspondence' or 'distance learning' courses to thwart student gatherings and campus protests. Distance learning law courses were opened to any high school graduate who passed the standard state exam. Large numbers of women, even in rural areas, seized the opportunity to obtain a legal education. In 1975 alone, approximately 6500 law students were admitted into the new correspondence program. Graduates of this program quickly became the majority of the Burmese legal profession.

Widespread protests in 1988 prompted a declaration of martial law and the closure of Burmese universities for three years. Government decrees also required law to be taught in English with most materials provided in English. To prevent protests, law departments were created at 'remote and newly built universities' further from the center of Yangon. Ultimately, Rangoon University was closed to all but a trickle of graduate students.

While the military regime restored a nominally civilian, professional judiciary in 1988, the system of governmental control over the judiciary remained unchanged. New judges were educated in the same manner as lawyers, with minimal training in Burmese law and procedure.

* * * * * * * *

As a result of military control and interference, the Burmese legal system is the antithesis of the rule of law. Corruption is endemic, due process principles are seldom observed in the courtroom, and judicial and prosecutorial independence in Myanmar is essentially non-existent. Burmese judges view themselves "as administrators rather than arbiters, basing decisions on state policy, instead of legal reasoning and precedent".

On the surface, trials in Myanmar follow the adversarial system. Below the surface, state actors control virtually every aspect of the system. Criminal prosecutions are conducted by 'law officers', working under the Attorney General, who in turn is closely aligned with the government. Law officers frequently act on political orders, prosecuting without regard to proper procedures or sufficient evidence. One report concluded: "The police often play a detrimental role in 'political' cases, partaking in or allowing corruption, fabrication of evidence, courtroom delays, politically motivated investigations and prosecutions, denial of access to clients, and the undermining of the presumption of innocence."

Economic corruption among judges and prosecutors is likewise pervasive. Where political or military interests are not at risk, judges routinely wring bribes from litigants. Prosecutors may help negotiate judicial bribes and share the proceeds. Even court functionaries join in, since their cooperation is required to meet with detained clients, access information, or enforce a judgment.

The organized legal profession is of little help. Bar Council members are hand-picked by the military. Politically active lawyers become targets for suspension, disbarment or worse. Lawyers opposing or challenging powerful state or private interests, may face contempt, criminal charges, or disbarment.

* * * * * * * *

Burmese lawyers must operate in this system. The vast majority studied law through correspondence courses or at one of the new law faculties. Their education was characterized by low enrollment qualifications, unqualified professors, and a narrow and outdated curriculum. Few students are proficient in English, limiting their comprehension of the lectures and materials. To pass examinations, students simply memorize English language exam questions and answers.

After graduation, Burmese lawyers are licensed as either 'advocates' or 'pleaders'. Advocates may appear in all tribunals, while pleaders are limited to District and Township Courts. Pleaders may be 'High Grade' and 'Second Grade' pleaders, with the latter limited to handling less serious criminal matters and low-level civil disputes. Many pleaders make no effort to become an advocate. Burma is the poorest country in Southeast Asia. Poverty, underdevelopment, and internal conflict impact lawyers and clients alike. Lawyers often are unable to afford the fees and costs associated with obtaining and maintaining an advocate's license. Consequently, lawyers – particularly women – often remain pleaders, working in their local communities throughout their professional lives.

As a result of these factors, unlike many countries, Myanmar has relatively large numbers of lawyers. In 2014, the UNDP reported that Myanmar had 9,000 licensed advocates with 2,000 in active practice, and 40,000 licensed high-grade pleaders with 15,000 in active practice. Statistics for second grade pleaders are simply unavailable.

Most of these Burmese lawyers engage in a second-class, subsistence practice. The Burmese court system for decades was controlled by the military and is notoriously corrupt. To obtain favorable treatment, lawyers typically bribe or otherwise influence the Court by extrajudicial means. Older lawyers often establish and jealously guard these relationships. Clients want lawyers with the ability to obtain favorable treatment. Young lawyers, even those with substantial talent, are frozen out of the system and left to years of menial tasks, without ever gaining actual courtroom experience.

Though the vast majority of lawyers in Myanmar are generalists, most handle cases involving land issues. Disputes over land arise when farmers and minority communities clash with the large corporate enterprises backed by the military, the government, and foreign interests. Burmese lawyers, given lack of resources and systemic corruption in the judiciary, face huge challenges when they walk into the courtroom.

Despite recent efforts at reform, little progress has been made. Relations between judges and lawyers in Myanmar remain adversarial, with little mutual respect. Clients see lawyers as 'brokers' with police, witnesses, court clerks, opposing counsel, and judges. According to some, a lawyer's acumen, analytical skills, and advocacy are irrelevant, because decisions are based on bribery or influence, not the law. Lawyers, in fact, may be viewed as an obstacle to striking an advantageous deal.

* * * * * * * *

With the modest easing of governmental repression in Myanmar, the usual dance began. Numerous international and national legal assistance programs swarmed the country. Assessments abounded as Burmese quickly tired of being repeatedly 'assessed' with no noticeable action.

When legal assistance programs did begin, many worked with the 'Old Guard' leadership. A number of assistance providers opted to work with the governmental officials, judge and Bar leaders who had been part of the system for decades. High-level conferences were held in Yangon and Nay Pyi Taw to discuss large-scale systemic changes in the legal system, attended by polite but ultimately intransigent Burmese officials. Ambitious visions, strategies and timelines were adopted, though few were pursued.

In some instances, the 'technical' assistance was directed at furthering the interests of the donors or the ruling elite. Countries eager to develop commercial ties and influence tilted their assistance to curry favor with those in power. Even ostensibly technical assistance in drafting new legislation, in fact, solidified the legal basis for foreign interests and the Burmese elite at the expense of farmers and minorities.

* * * * * * * *

At the other end of the spectrum, were tens of thousands of lawyers and millions of potential clients. Without financial resources or political power, they struggled to deal with the day-to-day, often life-and-death issues that plague Myanmar.

Many issues involve land rights and land tenure. Given the fundamental importance of property rights to most citizens in Myanmar, access to the courts to deal with such issues has major implications for the overall stability of the country. 'Land grabbing' cases deal – in different forms – with the usurpation of traditional lands by the government and military. Through various mechanisms, foreign interests and Burmese elites have effectively deprived many individuals and communities of their lands. Many instances have been reported in which farmers and entire communities have been dispossessed by the military, to make way for various economic development schemes run by cronies and/or foreign investors.

Laws have been created, often with the assistance of foreign experts, to legitimize these takings. Other mechanisms deprive the victims of any legal assistance or redress. Even where lawyers can become involved, the pervasive corruption and cronyism that characterizes governance in Myanmar typically turns the procedures into a sham.

* * * * * * * *

Sometimes, you must choose. While situations vary from country to country, the overriding factor in any rule of law program is the commitment to reform of the indigenous participants. Flashy programs directed at an indifferent or hostile audience, no matter how powerful or prestigious, do little to advance the rule of law. The critical component is whether the in-county participants will use the assistance to push for change.

Looking out at the mostly young faces in Mandalay, it was apparent that we had made the correct choice. These lawyers – mostly first and second-degree pleaders – were the legal system's ambassadors to tens of millions of Burmese peasants and poor. Their attitudes and actions would shape the public

161

face of the law at a personal level, far more effectively than any ministerial level conference in the remote capital.

On the surface, their challenges appeared insurmountable. Bereft of resources, and facing a perverted system controlled by the military and their moneyed allies, these lawyers seldom had opportunities to practice their profession in a legitimate fashion. Many were correspondence school graduates and had never even attended a class with a live instructor.

The trial skills program that we offered in Mandalay was a hands-on learning experience unknown in the Burmese legal education system. Some young lawyers travelled hours from the countryside to participate in the program. Adapted to fit the Burmese circumstances from program developed by the National Institute of Trial Advocacy in the United States, the course challenged these inexperienced Burmese lawyers to learn and hone their skills in witness examination and advocacy.

As we approached the course, we were unsure if the authorities would intervene. While Myanmar had opened a crack, the changes were painfully incremental. Lawyers continued to be under scrutiny, and every day stories appeared about Burmese who were arrested for pushing the limits too far. Invitations were by word of mouth; no press or publicity was sought. Program content was benign, based on skills rather than substance. Authorities were aware but tolerant of the program, so long as no anti-regime content was included.

Often tentative at first, young men and women tried their hands at various trial skills, often for the first time. The pace and intensity quickly picked up as participants realized that – at least in this setting – they could question the 'policeman' and other state witnesses without retribution. Arguments based on a logical explanation of the evidence, with strategies debated among the various teams, were presented to the handful of senior lawyers who served as 'judges'. Mistakes were made, often to uproarious laughter, yet the sense of shared purpose remained evident. Carefully, yet unmistakably, ethical issues were brought to the surface and discussed.

Many young people wondered aloud if such skills could ever become actually relevant in the Burmese courts. When asked what reform they would most like to see introduced in their local system, one team agreed that it would be to require a judge to return bribes received from the losing party. After years living in the system, they didn't want to set their sights too high.

At the same time, participants were excited at the prospect of gaining skills that someday might be relevant in a reformed Burmese court system. Second-grade pleaders – the lowest of the low – reveled in the chance to try their hand at polishing trial skills seldom, if ever, used in real world Myanmar. Cautious questions were asked about potential strategies to use legal acumen for the benefit of their thousands of clients devastated by the ongoing 'land grabbing' in the name of economic development. Lights came on for practitioners who seldom saw even a glimmer in the darkness of military rule.

* * * * * * * *

Was this exercise a pointless effort? After all, no one of us had any illusions that once the weekend was over, these young lawyers would suddenly start winning cases against powerful forces simply by brilliant cross-examination and oratory. Moreover, working with those at the bottom of the hierarchy, typically, is not glamorous; often it is hard work. Immediately quantifiable results probably will not be confirmed by some statistical metric.

At the same time, experience has shown that years of high-level dinners, meetings, and conferences with disinterested officials generated platitudes, but seldom any meaningful change. Worse, in some cases the assistance was used to either create a façade of reform, or to improve the efficiency of a repressive regime.

Unquestionably, improvements in the rule of law require systemic change. But where the leadership is resistant or where the changes are fragile (see Russia), systemic change may be generational. The agents of change may not be the governmental, judicial, or Bar leadership. Instead, change may ultimately come when young men and women – today's students, young judges, and street lawyers – begin moving into positions of authority.

At the same time, street lawyers and first-instance judges are the initial points of contact with the legal system for ordinary citizens. The attitudes, skills, and ethics of those practitioners telegraph the system's values to the public. Reform can be bottom up, not necessarily top down. As the American experience has shown, unheralded lawyers and judges from obscure venues may produce change where powerful leaders choose not to tread.

* * * * * * * *

The world's focus in the early 1990s was on the embryonic East and Central European democracies. Eventually, electoral democracy came quickly, but the legitimate adherence to the rule of law lagged in a number of countries. Those reared under old regimes learned the language of reform, but quietly adhered to many of the principles internalized under decades of authoritarian thought.

A quarter-century later, the young students, judges, and lawyers of the 1990s have begun to move into positions of authority. Improvements in the adherence to the rule of law – often painfully incremental – are gradually transforming these societies. Yet even in the heart of Europe, in countries with prosperous, well-educated populations and histories of democratic values, these modest advances have taken a generation.

Experience teaches that the rule of law will come even more slowly in countries in far less hospitable neighborhoods, with histories and cultures devoid of democratic traditions. True reform will take hold when generations of leaders are raised in democratic systems and slowly exert their influence over both their country's legal system and larger public.

Look at nearly any democratic country: the largest contingent of governmental leaders are trained in the law. One primary goal of legal assistance programs should be to begin the long process of developing these leaders. Particularly where authoritarianism remains entrenched, this process may be laborious, with progress nearly invisible. Yet, too often, assistance providers ignore younger women and men at the bottom of the pecking order.

* * * * * * * *

When the last witnesses were examined, and the last arguments were made, certificates were handed out one at a time to gleeful Burmese participants. Like their European counterparts two decades before, most sought personal photos with the faculty, adding my image to scores of cell phones across Myanmar. Even the minder asked for a photo with me, though it was unclear whether it was for his own edification or some police intelligence file.

In broken English or through translators, many of the young people offered heartfelt – occasionally tearful – thanks for the chance to participate. For many, it was their first opportunity to learn about their profession face-to-face with more experienced lawyers who actually enjoyed teaching and working with them. Perhaps more important, the workshops provided a safe space for these young people to discuss, even in a guarded fashion, many of the issues facing the legal system in their country.

When certificates had been distributed and all of the photos had been taken, two young women asked if we instructors would sit in chairs at the front of the room. Puzzled, we sat down in the plastic lawn chairs that had been gathered for that purpose. To our great chagrin, our students gathered in front of us, went to their knees, and bowed in unison. As we protested, our local translator asked us to be still. Such actions were a symbol, she said, reserved for those teachers whom students held in the highest respect.

We waved from the balcony as the young people in groups of two or three mounted motorbikes, or crawled into the beds of pickup trucks, and headed back to their villages. No one knows if any of them will someday be leaders in a democratic Myanmar. No metric yet developed can gauge if those days spent in a steamy classroom achieved any meaningful progress toward reform.

Yet the young people we worked with in Eastern Europe twenty-five years before, were now Ministers of Justice, judges on the European Court of Human Rights, and lawyers, prosecutors, and judges moving through the ranks of their countries' professions. Case by case, client by client, they have begun to demonstrate to the citizenry that the law can be fair and work to their benefit.

Some no-longer-young lawyers from the new Europe joined me on that balcony, working with young people in this generation's newly emerging democracies. The successes in the Balkans and Central Europe, won by their hard work and sacrifices over the past two and a half decades, suggest that these Burmese young people can likewise inch their country down the long path toward the rule of law.

The plastic chairs and shabby tables of the Takafuji beckoned, holding the promise of an iced-down Burmese beer. Sometimes, small things do matter.

Atty. Bill Meyer with a small group at a program in Myanmar.

Chapter 11

The Brandeis Institute for International Judges Fifteen Years On:
Promoting Cross-Court Dialogue and a Shared Professional Identity

Dr. Leigh Swigart

A group of judges sits around a large table, engaged in intense conversation. Their physical attributes and speech patterns suggest that they come from diverse regions of the world – Europe, Africa, the Americas, and Asia. Men predominate in the gathering but a few feminine voices can be heard as the judges contribute, in turn, their views on the topic under discussion. These individual views have been shaped by multiple factors, including the judges' country of origin, legal system and training, past professional activities, and current experience with an international court or tribunal. The tone of the conversation is collegial, the atmosphere spirited, and the setting, one that ensures confidentiality, as participants describe, with perhaps unaccustomed candor, the challenges as well as achievements of their unique work.

This is the Brandeis Institute for International Judges (BIIJ), a program created in 2002 for the benefit of the expanding number of judges who serve on the benches of international courts and tribunals. Some of these institutions have geographic jurisdictions that extend across the globe, such as the International Court of Justice (ICJ), International Tribunal for the Law of the Sea (ITLOS), and International Criminal Court (ICC). Others have jurisdictions limited to particular regions or sub-regions, such as the Inter-American Court of Human Rights (IACtHR), East African Court of Justice (EACJ), or the Caribbean Court of Justice (CCJ). The subject matter jurisdictions of these institutions are also varied, ranging from human rights, to war crimes, crimes against humanity and genocide, to inter-state dispute resolution and issues of regional integration. Within all this diversity, the judges sitting on the courts have a powerful common purpose – they all apply international law with the aim of creating a more peaceful and just world.

The concept underlying the BIIJ is simple and yet strikingly novel. The institutes provide members of the international judiciary with a rare opportunity to meet and discuss critical issues concerning the theory and practice of international justice, share their common experiences, unique challenges, and distinct approaches to their work, and reflect on the practical challenges as well as philosophical aspects of their profession through frank and open dialogue.

> This chapter will serve as a reflection on the BIIJ and its evolution over almost fifteen years of existence. How is the institute organized and who attends it? What topics are addressed, how are they selected, and which ones are of recurring interest? What do participants say they take away from the institute? What have been its successes, and which goals of the institute have yet to be fully realized? As the principal BIIJ planner and organizer, I appreciate this opportunity to think back over the various sessions of the institute and take stock of the program's overall performance.[23]

An anthropologist by training, I also consider it a privilege to have learned about the intricacies of international law and justice through designing a program for, and being privy to the confidential conversations of, individuals who could be considered the wise elders of this little-known 'culture'.

What exactly is the Brandeis Institute for International Judges?

---

[23] This chapter draws on my personal experiences as well as an in-depth evaluation of the BIIJ carried out in 2010 by international legal expert Karen Naimer. I am grateful for the input of my principal BIIJ collaborators: Linda Carter, Richard Goldstone, and Daniel Terris.

Since 2002, the International Center for Ethics, Justice, and Public Life (the Center) at Brandeis University [24] has brought together judges from the world's most active international courts and tribunals eleven times, for a period of four to five days each. The institutes have occurred approximately every 18 months, scheduled during the rare moments when the different institutions can each spare a member or two of their benches. The meetings have been convened in diverse locales in Europe, Africa, the United States, and the Caribbean.[25]

The impetus for the creation of the BIIJ came from discussions between the leaders of the Center, newly established at Brandeis University in 1998, and a member of its inaugural International Advisory Board, Richard Goldstone. Anyone familiar with the international justice sphere will immediately recognize this name. Goldstone served as Prosecutor of the International Criminal Tribunal for the former Yugoslavia (ICTY) and the International Criminal Tribunal for Rwanda ICTR), often referred to collectively as the United Nations (UN) Ad Hoc Tribunals. These were the first war crimes tribunals to be created since the Nuremberg and Tokyo tribunals, and they set the stage for the establishment of later international criminal institutions, most notably the International Criminal Court (ICC). [26]

Goldstone had previously served as a judge in his native South Africa and subsequently became a justice of its new Constitutional Court, established after the dismantlement of

---

[24] See http://www.brandeis.edu/ethics/index.html.

[25] For summaries and reports of all past institutes, see http://www.brandeis.edu/ethics/internationaljustice/biij/.

[26] For more about the early years of the ICTY and ICTR, see the interview transcripts collected through Brandeis University's Ad Hoc Tribunals Oral History Project:
http://www.brandeis.edu/ethics/internationaljustice/oral-history/index.html. An interview with Richard Goldstone is available at
http://www.brandeis.edu/ethics/internationaljustice/oral-history/interviews/goldstone.html.

Apartheid. The BIIJ grew out of a perceived need to create a forum for judicial dialogue in the international sphere. It was also, in many ways, a natural extension of seminars that Brandeis University had previously organized for members of United States state judiciaries (and later other professions), an activity inspired by the distinguished career of the University's namesake, Justice Louis Brandeis of the United States Supreme Court.[27]

The central aim of the BIIJ is to facilitate the means for international judges to strengthen judicial networks across regional and international courts and tribunals. National judges have frequently enjoyed the opportunity to forge and strengthen such networks, but prior to the establishment of the BIIJ, there were few, if any, mechanisms for globally dispersed international judges to dialogue with colleagues, despite the fact that they were often grappling with similar challenges in the field. Even today, fifteen years after its founding, there are no comparable programs of a continuous nature that bring together sitting international judges with their colleagues from other international courts and tribunals in a strictly off-the-record environment, allowing for an unusual mix of frankness and collegiality. The BIIJ has been made possible largely through grants from private foundations, and more recently, through cost sharing by partner institutions.

There are several unique aspects to the BIIJ. First, it brings together judges from vastly differing fields of law. Brandeis University took a risk in designing a program for judges from such disparate areas – encounters among lawyers and judges who share a professional background and training are instead the norm in the legal sphere. Over the years, international judges have expressed surprise and pleasure at the opportunity to engage with their counterparts from courts and tribunals addressing a wide variety of legal matters, and to learn how much overlap there is in their thinking and work.

---

[27] See
https://www.brandeis.edu/ethics/about/projects/past/seminars/index.html.

Second, the Brandeis Institute is unique in format, which has remained essentially unchanged over the years. Discrete sessions, linked to the overarching theme of that year's institute, are led by a leader or two co-leaders who have carefully conceptualized the topic to fit the interests of participants and 'assigned' them short preparatory readings – legal articles, excerpts from judgments, commentaries by legal experts, and so on. In the past, participants were sent through the mail a large binder with the institute materials at least a month in advance of the institute. More recently, the readings have been made available electronically. All participants must be able to read and speak English with some facility. While this requirement would seem to limit the pool of judges who can take part, the status of English as an official or working language of most international courts means that, for all practical purposes, the overwhelming majority of international judges are already proficient in that language.

Third, and very importantly, the BIIJ is unique in that the number of participants at any given institute is kept purposely small, averaging around fifteen judges per institute. Formality is also shunned – judges wear casual clothing and drop all titles, instead addressing one another with first names. All this makes for an intimate and easy atmosphere, which in turn encourages full engagement by everyone and formation of a professional network.

In the early years of the institute, session leaders were often academics and experts from the UN or other international organizations. Over time, leaders began to be drawn more from the pool of participants themselves, especially from among judges who had already attended the BIIJ at least once, and therefore understood how it was organized and what it was seeking to achieve. This change strengthened the sense of the event being 'for and by international judges'. Sessions have also been led by the Brandeis University conveners – myself and Center Director Daniel Terris included – and BIIJ co-directors. Richard Goldstone has held the latter position for each of the eleven institutes held to date, with Linda Carter, of the University of the Pacific McGeorge School of Law, acting as his co-director for eight of these sessions. It would be difficult to overestimate how much their personal knowledge of international law and practice, along with their warm collegiality, have made working on the BIIJ a personal high point of my career.

The hallmark of the BIIJ is its extended discussion time. Session leaders make introductory remarks to the group for a maximum of 30 minutes. The remainder of each topical session – between 90 and 120 minutes – is then devoted to discussion among judges, prompted by a set of questions from the leaders. This is the time when participants delve more deeply into the topic at hand, bringing forth their own experiences on the bench, their best practices, and sometimes their misgivings and failures. Moderators ensure that judges keep their individual contributions short so that there is ample time for everyone to weigh in, and they are invited to make further comments once everyone has had an initial opportunity to speak. Over the years, Brandeis has learned that having fewer and longer sessions constitute the optimal model; in other words, the quantity of topics is best sacrificed for the quality of discussions. Judges have expressed frustration in the past when insufficient time has been set aside to explore a topic in all its complexity.

Other details of the BIIJ enhance its discussion-based format. The institute is usually held in a pleasant and airy room, with lots of natural light but little technology. Judges sit around a large table, as do the session leaders. There is no 'head table' or dais distinguishing participants by role. Judges move from session discussions to coffee breaks and later to meals as a group. Often, they make an afternoon excursion together to a local historical site or other place of interest. Over the days of the institute, participants come to know and trust one another, they share experiences both inside and outside of the formal discussion space, and they develop close professional acquaintanceships – even friendships – that they can draw upon in the future.

It is also crucial, as intimated above, that institute discussions remain confidential so that judges may speak openly. Although Brandeis University has occasionally received requests from NGOs, government officials, or researchers to join the institute as observers – such a gathering does pique the curiosity of outsiders – such requests have not been granted. Judges agree that the presence of others would discourage the kind of frank dialogue they so value. The proceedings of the institutes are not, however, kept from the public. Notes are taken throughout the various session discussions and Brandeis subsequently prepares a report, [28] without attribution of comments or viewpoints to specific participants. Judges furthermore have the opportunity to read a draft of the report to ensure that there is nothing that inadvertently associates them with a particular statement, which might have negative consequences if it is controversial or critical.

Finally, in order that the larger public might benefit from the BIIJ in the various places where it is hosted, the institute often includes a public event. Sometimes, this is a keynote address by an eminent participant, such as the UN Under Secretary General for Legal Affairs.[29] Other times, the event might be a round table or panel discussion, featuring a couple of international judges along with local academics or government figures. For example, BIIJ 2015, which took place in Malta, included a public roundtable exploring the challenges associated with contemporary migration to Malta and other parts of southern Europe. Speakers included an international judge, legal scholars and a Maltese government representative, and members of the academic, civil society, and migrant communities were in attendance.

Who participates in the BIIJ?

From its inception, the BIIJ has sought a wide representation of international courts and tribunals among its participants. There have been 'regulars' on its institutional invitation list: the two Ad Hoc Tribunals, European Court of Human Rights (ECtHR), European Court of Justice (ECJ), IACtHR, ICC, ICJ, ITLOS, and the World Trade Organization

---

[28] I am largely in charge of report preparation but often receive critical assistance from note takers, who are usually legal experts themselves. Co-director Linda Carter has also been particularly active in the process of editing and perfecting the report.

[29] Three persons holding this position have participated in the BIIJ: Hans Corell in 2002 on the Brandeis campus in Waltham, Massachusetts; Nicolas Michel in 2009 in Trinidad; and Patricia O'Brien in 2010 in Salzburg, Austria.

Appellate Body (WTO AB). Several institutions have come into operation since the institute was established and have joined the ranks, such as the African Court of Human and Peoples' Rights (ACtHPR), CCJ, Extraordinary Chambers in the Courts of Cambodia (ECCC), and Special Tribunal for Lebanon (STL). Other institutions that once participated in the BIIJ have seen their mandates completed and thus are no longer present. This is the case the Special Court for Sierra Leone (SCSL) and more recently the ICTR (with the ICTY soon to follow). A couple of regional courts – the Andean Tribunal of Justice (ATJ) and the East African Court of Justice (EACJ) – have participated only once, but Brandeis hopes to see them become regular attendees in the future. The Mechanism for International Criminal Tribunals (MICT), the body established to take care of residual matters for the Ad Hoc Tribunals, will also be a regular participant moving forward.

The wide variety of institutions participating in the BIIJ makes for a diverse group of judges around the discussion table in terms of nationality, legal system, background, and professional experience. This diversity is a critical component of the institute, affording a range of viewpoints that one would not normally find in a gathering of judges from a single country or even region. Brandeis has sought to include women judges in the institute to the extent possible. However, given that the decision about which judge will attend the BIIJ has largely been made by an international court's president, and furthermore, that there is an extreme gender imbalance on most of these institutions' benches,[30] BIIJ organizers have never been able to achieve a balance of men and women around the table.

Over the years, Brandeis has come to appreciate the importance of our 'repeat participants'. Indeed, the ideal group for any given institute has proven to be one where one-third to one-half of the participants has already attended at least once.

---

[30] International courts with explicit language in their statutes requiring fair or adequate gender representation on the bench, like the ICC and ACtHPR, have predictably higher percentages of women. See Nienke Grossman, Achieving Sex-Representative International Court Benches, 110 Am. J. Int'l L. 82 (2016).

Some have returned multiple times, for example Hisashi Owada (Japan) of the ICJ, Theodor Meron (U.S.A.) of the ICTY and MICT, and Sophia Akuffo (Ghana) of the ACtHPR, among many others. Fausto Pocar (Italy) of the ICTY holds the attendance record; he has attended all eleven institutes and been a frequent session leader as well. A particularly interesting category of repeat participant is made up of judges who first attended while serving on one court, and later attended when attached to another with a distinctly different jurisdiction. Erik Møse (Norway) was once judge and president of the ICTR, a criminal tribunal, and later attended as a judge of the ECtHR, a human rights court. Dennis Byron (St. Kitts & Nevis) was also once judge and president of the ICTR before moving on to serve as judge and president of the CCJ, a court of economic integration with an additional appellate jurisdiction in the Caribbean. And Sanji Monageng (Botswana) attended originally while serving on the African Commission on Human and Peoples' Rights[31] and later participated several times as a criminal judge with the ICC. The breadth of experience of such judges is remarkable, and their capacity to compare different legal frameworks as well as institutional practices and arrangements contributes greatly to institute discussions.

Our ongoing contact with international judges led me in the mid 2000's to a book project focused on this professional group. Written with my colleagues Cesare P.R. Romano and Daniel Terris, *The International Judge: An Introduction to the Men and Women Who Decide the World's Cases*[32] explores a wide range of issues, including the varied backgrounds of this group, how they reach the international bench, what their experiences are like inside their courts and tribunals, and how politics comes into play in the international judicial sphere. One of the aims of the book project was to inform the public about who international judges are and how they carry out their critical work. We believed that during a period in American political life characterized by hostility toward international

---

[31] Before the African Court of Human and Peoples' Rights was established, Brandeis invited participants from the Commission to attend the institute.

[32] Brandeis University Press and Oxford University Press, 2007.

organizations, in particular the ICC, such a book could reassure readers that international judges were not 'unaccountable', but instead well-trained and experienced practitioners committed to judicial standards, although working outside of a domestic context.

What do international judges talk about?

At the heart of the BIIJ are the topical sessions around which the whole event is organized. The overarching theme of each institute is generally inspired by the closing session of the preceding one. Participants weigh in on what they found useful about the BIIJ just being concluded, and make suggestions about the format, scheduling, pre-institute communication, follow-up, and so on for future gatherings. International judges are also asked what topics they think might be usefully discussed at future institutes.

It was just such a conversation that gave rise, for example, to a series of interconnected themes over three separate institutes: 'Toward an International Rule of Law' in 2010 (Salzburg, Austria); 'The International Rule of Law: Coordination and Collaboration in Global Justice' in 2012 (Carmona, Spain); and 'The International Rule of Law in a Human Rights Era' in 2013 (Lund, Sweden). The original interest in the notion of an international rule of law was expressed at the closing session of BIIJ 2009 (Port of Spain, Trinidad). Participants noted that throughout the days of the 2009 institute, there had been recurring references to what they viewed as an evolving sense of the power of international law and respect for its mandates. This idea was expanded, and its 'reality' tested in relation to different areas of law and types of jurisdictions, at the following three institutes.

As for the individual topical sessions that make up the institutes, they can generally be grouped under a few rubrics: the international rule of law and global justice (which includes the relationship of international and domestic jurisdictions); politics and international justice; judicial ethics in the international sphere; the impact of diversity on the work of international judges; and challenges to the development of international justice and its institutions.[33] In the early years of the BIIJ, the organizers included some sessions that approached the field of international justice in a more interdisciplinary fashion, for example by using literature or historical documents as an oblique way of reflecting on the law and legal practice. This did not end up being a popular approach, however; participants expressed the need for more direct discussion of issues that they faced on a daily basis, along with 'nuts and bolts' aspects of judicial work. Despite this resistance to the 'unconventional', organizers have continued to include sessions exploring how diversity – cultural, legal, linguistic, etc. – plays out in international justice. Although this may be an unaccustomed field of inquiry for many international judges, the fact that their institutions, almost by definition, bring together individuals from disparate parts of the globe, with different worldviews and ways of expressing them, makes a regular discussion of diversity *de rigueur*, at least in the eyes of the organizers.

Sessions addressing common ethical issues faced by international judges are also a regular offering. Many of these issues are the same ones encountered by judges at the domestic level, such as concerns about ensuring impartiality and independence. The international sphere presents judges with some unique challenges, however, and these have been explored more than once over the eleven institutes. The appointment or election procedures for international judgeships often begin, for example, with nomination by a national government. Judges serving on inter-state dispute resolution bodies or human rights courts may find themselves in a delicate position if their own state is party to a case they are adjudicating, particularly if they wish to be re-elected for a second term or find employment with their government after rotating off the international bench.[34] The question of which

---

[33] The most substantive session discussions that have occurred over the eleven institutes have been made available in individual pdf format at
http://www.brandeis.edu/ethics/internationaljustice/biij/BIIJ_articl es.html.
[34] For more on how different international courts handle the nationality of judges, see Leigh Swigart, "The 'National Judge':

'outside activities' are appropriate for part-time international judges to pursue has also been discussed several times.

After the first several BIIJ programs, the organizers decided to develop institute programs in consultation with a program committee comprising three or four BIIJ 'alumni', drawn from different types of international jurisdictions. These committee members ensure that the topics to be addressed at the upcoming institute are relevant and valuable to participants; indeed, working with a program committee serves to embed insider knowledge into the BIIJ 'curriculum'. Committee members also receive individual invitations to the upcoming institute – where they typically play the role of session leader – and thus do not deprive a colleague on their bench from attending in response to the institutional invitation.

Another important BIIJ innovation that came over time, was the establishment of break-out sessions for judges serving on courts with similar jurisdictions. Although the plenary nature of the institute is central to its character, participants occasionally observed, in the early years, that some discussions had to remain overly general if they were to apply to all categories of judges, or that they missed the opportunity to share concrete experiences and lessons with their colleagues from comparable institutions. In response to these observations, BIIJ organizers now include at least one long session in each institute program where judges from criminal courts, human rights courts, and inter-state dispute resolution bodies can discuss issues particular to their jurisdictions. These issues are decided ahead of time, with one participant acting as the 'break-out group coordinator' who communicates with his cohort to solicit their suggestions. In the past, criminal court judges have focused, for example, on how victim participation at the ICC raises challenges not experienced by the Ad Hoc Tribunals or the SCSL. Human rights judges have explored how their respective institutions monitor the implementation of their decisions by respondent states. And judges of inter-state dispute resolution bodies have compared the use of expert

Some Reflections on Diversity in International Courts and Tribunals". *University of the Pacific McGeorge Law Review* 42:1 (2010).

witnesses in cases and discussed whether it is better to have court-appointed or party-appointed experts.

Finally, it should be mentioned that when the BIIJ is co-hosted by a local entity, these partners often help shape the program to reflect their own areas of specialization. In 2013, scholars and practitioners associated with the Raoul Wallenberg Institute of Human Rights and Humanitarian Law (University of Lund, Sweden), led sessions under the institute theme 'The International Rule of Law in a Human Rights Era'. BIIJ 2015, co-hosted by the Faculty of Law of the University of Malta, devoted a session to the local impact of international justice, focusing on how ECtHR judgments were and were not having an effect on the migration crisis in the Mediterranean. And the iCourts Centre for Excellence on International Courts at the University of Copenhagen partnered with Brandeis in 2016 to explore the theme of the authority of international courts and tribunals, one of iCourts' principal research areas. Such partnerships have enriched the institute, kept the program from becoming repetitive, and opened up new and challenging areas of inquiry for participating judges.

What do participants say about the BIIJ?

In 2010, Brandeis University hired a consultant to perform an in-depth and independent evaluation of the BIIJ program, based largely on interviews with almost 50% of past participants. I confess to having felt some apprehension during this process. Would the enthusiasm expressed by international judges immediately following any given institute translate into a long-term appreciation? Would participants continue to feel the impact of the institute years after their experience? If so, what was the nature of this enduring impact?

The results of the evaluation were overwhelmingly positive, pointing to the continued need for this unique forum for international judges. The ensemble of interviews from 2010 indicated that the BIIJ impacts its participants in several distinct ways. These are illustrated below by the comments of selected judges, some of whom participated in institutes organized after the evaluation date.

The BIIJ strengthens a sense of professional community.

According to Georges Abi-Saab (Egypt),[35] the Brandeis institutes "are a very important vehicle of socialization, of cohesion, and of solidifying the community [of international judges], of contributing to its integration". Carmel Agius (Malta)[36] expressed a similar sentiment: At the BIIJ, there is "a general acknowledgment that you're not a technocrat. You don't walk into an international tribunal or court as a new judge and sit down, and you look at the sections in the law and the procedural code, or you hear the evidence, and you just apply one to the other and that's it. It takes more than that. That message came out at the institute." Nina Vajić (Croatia)[37] described a more personal aspect of attending the BIIJ: "There were some people whom I knew before going to the BIIJ. Of course, this deepened our friendship. But with some people, yes, I definitely made new contacts. It's also very important because you just create a kind of ... network. If someone [from the institute] came here, even in a year or two, of course I would treat him as an old friend, and I would do everything to accommodate him or her." Elsie Thompson (Nigeria)[38] summed up her experience in a nutshell: "In less than a week, I feel like I have a new judicial family."

The BIIJ reinforces judicial confidence.

This important impact was expressed powerfully by Jon Kamanda (Sierra Leone[39]): "We were the first court to really [consider] different aspects of sexual slavery, and bush wives and forced marriage. So, when you hear the comments of more seasoned judges, that they would have done it the same way, it gives you confidence that you are doing the right thing. You come back [to your court], and your colleagues also feel

---

[35] Former ad-hoc judge of the ICJ, former judge of the ICTY, and former member of the WTO AB. Attended BIIJ 2007.

[36] Judge and former president of the ICTY. Attended BIIJ 2007, 2013 and 2015.

[37] Former ECtHR judge. Attended BIIJ 2007, 2009, 2010, and 2012.

[38] Former ACtHPR judge. Attended BIIJ 2015.

[39] President and appeals judge of the Special Court for Sierra Leone. Attended BIIJ 2009 and 2010.

emboldened to do better work." András Sajó (Hungary) [40] remarked: "I really learned a lot, and it was a great support emotionally, for me to hear that judges in other institutions face similar problems."

The BIIJ creates a space for introspection and sharing of knowledge.

Fausto Pocar (Italy)[41] said this of the work of international judges: "We have a limited time for reflection in international courts ... So, having a few days in which you just concentrate on these issues, instead of thinking through your daily work, inevitably allows you to reflect ... And through the discussion with colleagues, maybe you go back and say, 'Well, this is something I should keep in mind.' This is the ideal in any profession, I think, to have more time to reflect on what one does." Rowan Downing (Australia)[42] remarked: "Not only were the topics relevant to my work as an international judge, but meeting colleagues from a wide range of international courts and tribunals underscored how we all face common problems and challenges." The opportunity to meet judges from courts with similar jurisdictions also enhances the work of international judges. As Fatsah Ouguergouz (Algeria) [43] observed: "The human rights break-out sessions at the BIIJ were very fruitful. The African Court has much to learn from the European Court."

The BIIJ addresses ethical issues in the international sphere.

"Ethical discussions are like a mirror ... You hold it up to yourself and to the activity of any court, international or national." In this statement, Erik Møse (Norway)[44] notes that

---

[40] Former judge of the ECtHR. Attended BIIJ 2016.

[41] Appeals judge and former president of the ICTY. Attended all eleven institutes to date.

[42] Former judge of the ECCC. Current judge and president of the UN Dispute Tribunal. Attended BIIJ 2013 and 2015.

[43] Former judge of the ACtHPR. Attended BIIJ 2007, 2010, and 2016.

[44] Former judge and president of the ICTR. Current judge of the ECtHR. Attended BIIJ 2003, 2013, and 2015.

ethics are the cornerstone of judging in any system. Egils Levits (Latvia)[45] describes how a BIIJ discussion allowed him to reflect on ethics in practice: "In some [ethical] cases presented, I was surprised that there were such different views, because it seems to me that my view is obvious. And then I was expected to justify my position while other colleagues justified their position. It was very fruitful to get more insight and to see that what I think myself is not a given."

There is no other event quite like the BIIJ.

Jennifer Hillman (USA)[46] describes the value of the BIIJ from her point of view after attending it twice: "[The BIIJ] is utterly unique. I've been a long-time member of [a law association], and they have certainly had other occasions in which there have been a number of international law judges on a panel. But that is very different from getting you together behind closed doors, in private for your own edification ... I often have thought, in a lot of my various government roles, that as soon as you land one of these positions, the assumption is that you don't need any further training. And I think that's a very false assumption ... So, in that sense, I think it's fantastic to have something like the Brandeis Institute where judges can learn from one another and from other experiences." Navanethem Pillay (South Africa)[47] put it even more succinctly: "Judges derive enormous benefit from the dialogue that Brandeis helps to promote."

Not all BIIJ participants have been wildly enthusiastic, of course. Some might well believe that attending once is enough. However, the many international judges wishing to repeat the experience have led us to believe that we have found a winning formula. And when these judges serve long or repeated judicial terms in the international sphere, or move onto a second international court, the network building effect of the institute

---

[45] Judge of the European Court of Justice, former judge of the European Court of Human Rights. Attended BIIJ 2006 and 2009.

[46] Former member of the WTO AB. Attended BIIJ 2009, 2010, and 2012.

[47] Former judge and president of the ICTR. Former judge of the ICC. Former UN High Commissioner for Human Rights. Attended BIIJ 2002, 2003, 2004, 2006, and 2007.

multiplies across time and space. The BIIJ aim of helping international judges develop a professional identity – which results, in turn, in increased camaraderie and knowledge sharing across courts – is slowly but surely being realized.

What could the BIIJ do better in the future?

Despite the overall feeling that the BIIJ is successful, the organizers frequently tweak aspects of its format, structure, and planning from institute to institute, learning through trial and error. (The content is, of course, designed anew for each institute.) If I had to describe one goal of the BIIJ that remains elusive, it would be sustaining the positive energy and network building aspects of the event between institutes. Most participants leave the BIIJ full of renewed enthusiasm for both their profession and the benefits of interaction with their peers across courts. But how best to keep this feeling alive once judges return to their often crushing daily schedules of judicial work?

Unfortunately, Brandeis has not figured out the answer to this question. We have established electronic lists several times – at the request of participants, I might add – so that they might continue to share ideas, articles and judgments, or ask for assistance on questions of jurisprudence or practice. But there is never much traffic on the listserv and it eventually fades out due to disuse. We have also considered the organization of 'mini-institutes' – for judges living in a certain locale, for example – between the regular institutes, to keep up the momentum. But it is already a challenge to find funding for the BIIJ and supporting additional meetings would increase the fundraising pressure.

It is also difficult to gauge the impact of the institute reports that are so painstakingly edited, revised, laid out professionally with photos and 'pull quotes', and sent to all judges currently sitting on an international court or tribunal, as well as many experts in the international legal and NGO spheres. How often are the reports read and referenced? Does reading an account of an institute's proceedings allow non-participating judges to learn from the discussions? Does it enhance their feeling of belonging to a unique professional group? How can we best reach out to individuals who have joined the bench of an international court or tribunal for the first time and are unaware of the BIIJ? The circulation of the reports has been greatly enhanced by their simultaneous publication since 2010 in the University of the Pacific Law Review, which means they are accessible and searchable through major law databases.

As I move into the report preparation phase following our most recently organized BIIJ in 2016 in Copenhagen, I ponder this conundrum. We are convinced that the institutes serve an important purpose for members of the international judiciary, and that the judges who participate in them come away, in most cases, changed by the experience. The continuing challenge for the BIIJ is to get 'the biggest bang for our buck' by successfully extending the BIIJ experience, both for alumni after and between gatherings, and for judges who have not yet attended an institute.

Our quest for the best strategy continues.

Dr. Leigh Swigart with a group of participants in a Brandeis Institute for International Judges.

Dr. Swigart with a group of international judges in the courtroom
of the Caribbean Court of Justice in Port of Spa Spain, Trinidad,
which acted as local host of the 2006 institute.

An international group of judges from Senegal at the Brandeis
Institute.

Chapter 12

Judges of the World
Same Values, Same Challenges

Mr. Mokhtar Lakhdari – General Director of
Judiciary and Legal Affairs
Algerian Ministry of Justice

In March 2001, when I was selected to participate in a study trip to the United States of America, Algeria was in a process of a political and administrative reforms, which were decided by the President Abdelaziz Bouteflika after his election in April 1999, to give the country a new face after Years of terrorism and destruction that we went through it in 1990s.

Justice reform was one of the most important open workshops, where a national committee was set up to diagnose weaknesses in the judicial system and to make proposals and recommendations that enhance the role of the Judiciary in protecting rights and freedoms.

The study trip was organized by a non-governmental organization and whose main theme was 'strengthening the rule of law and supporting judiciary reform' through the American experience. During that period, I was in charge of the penal affairs in the ministry of justice, and this study trip was a valuable opportunity to learn about the United States of America and its legal system.

Before this trip, I had a divergent opinion about the United States of America, because of the different paradoxes in the modern history of the American nation. This young nation has broken away from the British Empire and made the values of freedom and democracy sacred. The same nation that spent her blood during the two world wars to defend "…the principles that gave her birth…" (President Wilson's War Message to Congress April 2, 1917.)

However, in the other part of the history, the USA launched a brutal war against the Vietnamese people; disrespected the civil rights of the African-Americans, and did not seek to find a fair solution to the Palestinian cause.

All those thoughts were in my mind when the plane landed at midday at Washington Dulles apnt on March 9, 2001. It was not my first trip abroad. I used to spend the summer holidays in Europe, but the United States always seemed to me something else. But most of all it was a priceless opportunity to interact with my fellow colleagues of my own country, lawyer, journalist and human rights activists and employees, because we would not have met if it wasn't for this trip.

The duty of reservation that is imposed on me by judicial profession and the position, as a Ministry of Justice official that I occupy would not have allowed me to exceed certain limits in my relations with them.

The dialogue that I had with the participants in this trip, and exchanging different positions on many issues (freedom of expression and death penalty...) allowed each of us to understand the other's justifications. Especially when we evoked the issue of how to deal with the remains of the tragedy, which Algeria went through during the years of terrorism, and what is the most compatible solution to international standards and human rights.

The journey lasted 15 days and we visited several states from the east, south and west. We traveled by air and by land. We saw wonderful and varied scenery. These were moments of reflection and observation.

If I could sum up all my thoughts in one sentence, it would be: The United States of America should not only be admired because of its military and economic potential, but also in its institutions and elites and in the principles on which the state was founded on, to ensure its greatness.

As I knew that the judicial system is the result of the political, social and historical conditions, this made me think about what can I bring to my country from this experience.

When I returned to Algeria, I was late in writing the usual report of the missions abroad, until the head of the minister's office came to my attention. I said to him: I'm puzzled and hesitated, in if I should write a volume or not to write anything at all. The truth is that I did not want to write only about issues related to the judiciary, but also about the social, cultural and political dimensions of this visit.

March 2001 was a turning point in my professional life as I changed my mind on many things. I remember that I was about to complete a master's thesis on the relationship of the judiciary to the press. I had to review the plan and devoted new chapters to integrate the American experience in my research: TV in the courtrooms; the offense of defamation and the principles provided by the American Constitution regarding those issues.

This was not the only benefit of this visit, but a reference experience to develop the cooperation programs with the American and international organizations that benefited many Algerian judges in different fields.

The visit was the starting point for the preparation of many cooperation programs between the ABA and the High School of Magistracy in Algeria, which allowed the US judges to lecture in Algeria on several topics, and build a bridge between Algerian and Americans judges, who despite their different surroundings, share the same values and the same challenges. That is the biggest lesson we learn from this international cooperation programs.

Director Mokhtar Lakhdari (Left), on an international panel.

Chapter 13
Endings
Attorney Mary Noel Pepys

Before my foray into international rule of law programs, I had described my life as a golden bore. However, since my first international assignment in Bulgaria, that boredom was replaced by exhilarating challenges, sheer satisfaction, and a constant renewal of hope.

Since 1993, I have worked in over 40 countries with not only USAID and its contractors, the World Bank and the United Nations Development Programme, but also the U.S. Department of State as the Justice Advisor at the U.S. Embassy in Afghanistan from 2008 to 2009. Throughout the past 24 years, I provided legal and technical assistance to national governments, judiciaries, legal profession, law faculties and civil society NGOs by implementing, managing, and evaluating rule of law programs.

While several rule of law projects which I supported have met their demise, I was delighted to visit Latvia in 2015 and learn that the LJTC has expanded its space from one small training room and an even smaller office in 1995, to three floors of training facilities and offices. It now has a staff of eight, conducts about 200 high quality-training seminars to judges, prosecutors, advocates, and lawyers, and receives approximately 160,000 Euros annually from the Latvian government.

While political will for the LJTC was strong in 1995, it waxed and waned over the years, but the judges were stalwart supporters of the LJTC and worked together to overcome political and financial challenges that arose throughout the years. Not only were the judges who led the JTC of high caliber, but also the staff, particularly the first and succeeding executive directors.

As there were other rule of law donors in Latvia also interested in developing the LJTC, particularly the United National Development Programme, the Soros Foundation Latvia, and the Constitutional and Legislative Policy Institute, all donors collaborated and shared the responsibilities of technical and financial assistance to the LJTC without any overlapping. This was the result of a few donors with a common purpose and flexible mandates. Equally important was that each donor had limited funds so that no donor could overpower the others by the sheer weight of its budget. Donor support to the LJTC continued until 2009 when the last ABA ROLI volunteer completed his term on the LJTC Council.

The LJTC's success is due, according to the first executive director and the current executive director of the LJTC, to a myriad of reasons since its creation. The first and most important was the initiative of the international donors to support Latvia in building its judicial training center, and the quality and coordination of their services. "Without such impetus, it would have been considerably longer before a continuing education program for judges would have been created in Latvia," stated the first executive director.

Secondly, European Union (EU) accession and the EU's expectation of the application of EU law in Latvia, as well as European donor funding provided to Latvia to enhance judicial qualifications, helped to convince the Latvian government to increase its financial support to the LJTC. According to a senior level Latvian judge, "One of the major reasons for the LJTC's success is that the judicial, executive, and legislative powers had a common understanding of the steps to take in order to build a rule of law state. Consequently, all judicial reforms were initiated and coordinated by the Ministry of Justice to ensure the needs of the Latvian government were being addressed by the donors."

Thirdly, the high level of constant and open communication between the staff of the LJTC and the legal and judicial communities in Latvia, including client satisfaction surveys, resulted in the development of training services that responded to the needs of judges, prosecutors, advocates, and lawyers. Further, the content of training courses was expanded from substantive law to skills-training such as oratory ability, decision writing techniques, judicial conduct, and managing a courtroom to reflect the public's expectations of judges and prosecutors.

Fourthly, the skills capacity of the staff, particularly programmatic and financial, was significantly enhanced throughout the years. Such that, today, four specialized lawyers who are skilled in adult-teaching methodologies are now program directors responsible for 200 seminars.

To put LJTC's progress in perspective, twenty-two years ago when I first worked in Latvia, laws and amendments to laws were not systematically distributed to the judiciary. The only way a judge could learn of a new law or an amendment was to buy a legal newspaper. One Latvian judge showed me his criminal code in which he had pasted the newspaper version of the amendments. His code looked more like an accordion than a legal text, and he couldn't even assure me that it was current. But it's all he had upon which to make 'informed' decisions.

Today, not only are all laws electronically distributed to all judges, but also LJTC's course materials and training sessions are available online. Informed judicial decisions have been transformed over the past two decades.

Latvia's success with the LJTC is a direct outgrowth of the laissez-faire approach to international rule of law assistance in the early 90s, during which rule of law development was left primarily to the determination of individuals.

Today, developing the rule of law has become big business, and is prescriptively directed by governments, international donors, and contractors with considerable regulations and bureaucratic tangles. While a systematic approach to developing the rule of law is fundamental in order to ensure consistency, there are drawbacks. Among many, one of the most important is the lack of flexibility. In emerging democracies where the stability of the country and its governmental institutions are in flux, key local decision-makers, upon which donor contractual agreements and expectations are often based, can be unpredictable given the insecurity of their political positions. Under these circumstances, the rule of law practitioner attempting to implement the contractual work plan is stymied. There is often little flexibility to accommodate changing circumstances. In fact, predetermined planning and unnecessary restrictions and limitations not only impede adaptability, but also dumbs down rule of law practitioners who are thwarted from capitalizing upon their expertise.

While the wild west, or more appropriately wild east, approach in developing the rule of law in the early 90s may have its critics, it allowed for rule of law practitioners to address in a timely manner a country's legitimate needs proffered by its leadership rather than by donor institutions, which have their own missions to accommodate as well as lengthy bureaucratic planning processes. The early 90s rule of law development allowed for immediate and creative responses to meet unexpected situations, as rule of law practitioners were able to use their own ingenuity to create solutions in order to overcome unforeseen barriers.

This is not to say that everyone who joined the rule of law bandwagon in the early 90s was of high caliber. There were, indeed, misfits who should have never left the U.S. But there were few, as there are today. According to several Bulgarian judges, "The best rule of law practitioners over the years were those who were devoted to their mission and who adapted to the traditions and culture of the country, while the worst ones were those who demonstrated complete ignorance of the country's legal system and did not appreciate nor respect local traditions. Furthermore, there were some rule of law practitioners who believed they were superior to local legal professionals and would only work with high-level governmental officials. As a result, they accomplished very little."

According to a Latvian judge, "Some rule of law 'experts' did not acknowledge their counterparts as equal professionals, deeming local lawyers and judges as less educated and less skilled." As a result, "Some of the first seminars conducted by rule of law practitioners were useless and we lost time developing a training curriculum as Latvian judges did not want to waste time attending basic seminars." I remember a Bulgarian judge telling me that she and her colleagues would clap with false enthusiasm, as if they were thrilled to learn fundamental legal issues, for they did not want to offend the 'expert' who was clueless as to the educational level of Bulgarian judges. These instances, luckily, were rare.

Rule of law practitioners, then and now, are not the only ones subject to critical review by my Bulgarian and Latvian colleagues, as they also commented on their own judges and attorneys. "Most were monolingual as they are today, and due to their limited language skills, one of the major reasons donor projects are implemented slowly is that all communications and trainings have to be provided in the local language, which is challenging as the substance and nuance of foreign legal concepts is difficult to translate."

When I began in the early 90s, times were euphoric for both the rule of law practitioner and the beneficiary. Years ago, however, much of that euphoria began to wear off. It began to subside once it became clear that developing the rule of law was not going to occur overnight, which many had hoped, but would take a generation or two.

It began to change once it became clear that promises made by rule of law donors were illusory and that commitments made by local legal professionals lacked political will. The beneficiaries became tried of meeting with successive donors, who would ask the same questions as their predecessors without any results, who appeared at times to meet only for the purpose of, in the words of one Latvian judge, 'ticking off their required meetings'. For some beneficiaries, it became a waste of time.

It also became a waste of time for some rule of law practitioners, who conducted obligatory meetings with legal professionals who had no intention of pursuing democratic reforms. I remember vividly sitting in the office of a high-ranking Serbian judge in the mid-90s, who extolled the virtues of an independent judiciary professing he had never taken a bribe, while being surrounded by exquisite furniture and European art. It was such a farce, particularly since he wasn't wise enough to recognize the absurdity of his comments while sitting amidst such luxury, which his paltry salary could ill afford.

But, he wasn't alone. Many of the recipients of rule of law assistance, while not naïve as the Serbian judge, were sufficiently savvy to learn the democratic lingo. In fact, it was not uncommon to meet a local legal professional who could espouse the benefits of democracy better than the practitioner, who knew that by saying the right words, financial support and technical assistance would pour in.

What have not changed, however, since the 90s, are the essential elements in developing the rule of law in emerging democracies. Whether rule of law practitioners act on their own initiative or as result of donors' mandates, the nature of developing the rule of law is similar in all countries, even those with vastly different political and legal systems, as the principles of judicial independence are international and transcend geographic borders.

The United Nations Basic Principles on the Independence of the Judiciary Seventh United Nations Congress on the Prevention of Crime and the Treatment of Offenders; the Council of Europe, Recommendation No. R (94) 12, 'On the Independence, Efficiency, and Role of Judges', dated 13 October 1994; and the European Charter on the Statute for Judges, set forth international standards which are fundamental to judicial independence. The major indicators of an independent judiciary which is guaranteed and protected by law are:

- State guarantees of an independent judiciary are provided for in the constitution and/or national laws;
- The judiciary has jurisdiction over matters affecting the human rights and civil liberties of its citizens;
- The judiciary has jurisdiction over the constitutionality of legislation and other governmental acts;
- The judiciary has exclusive authority to decide all matters within its jurisdiction; and
- The judiciary has the authority and respect of the executive and legislative branches, and the citizenry.

While these fundamental principles of judicial independence can be applied worldwide, the conditions within each country vary. The historical, cultural, and religious background of each country dictates different approaches with unique time constraints.

The justice system in each country has its own characteristics to which judges, attorneys, court personnel, as well as the political establishment have become accustomed and have accommodated. Not only does the justice system have to be restructured and infused with democratic principles, but also those who engage in the justice system must be retrained on their appropriate role within a democratic society. Often, such changes are the result of a robust civil society whose new awareness of its rightful role in demanding government reform and whose voices, silenced in the past, have become heard and respected.

Underlying a dysfunctional justice system is the element of corruption that takes various forms in each country. From buying judgeships that, in one country, reputedly cost as much as $300,000, to currying favor with governmental officials in whose hands a judge's future lays, or demanding cash from a litigant, or deciding a case based not on the merits but out of fear of retribution, these are just some of the causes of corruption that must be dealt with on a country by country basis.

The remedies to judicial corruption are as vast as the causes. The governance structure of the judiciary must ensure its significant authority, if not control, over the administration and budget of the courts and over the appointment and promotion process of judges. In corrupt countries, judges are often beholden to the president, Ministry of Justice, and/or parliamentarians, whose undue influence can detrimentally affect the quality of judicial services. Assuming control over the budgetary process of the courts insulates judges from the deleterious influence that other branches of government may have on the behavior of judges. Creating a judicial body, such as a judicial council with a majority of members as judges, which has responsibility for selecting and promoting judges based on objective criteria, can enhance the integrity of the judicial appointment process. Developing court administrative procedures that are clear and reduce obscurity, that are understandable by the court user, and are sufficiently precise to minimize discretion by the court staff, reduces the arbitrary application of court procedures, which is a fundamental cause of judicial corruption.

As the cornerstone of a government based on the rule of law is the independence of the judiciary, it is paramount in providing rule of law assistance, that the unique needs of each country are properly identified and take priority to the mission of the donor. While this principle is obvious, it is not uncommon for the strategic interests of the donor to overshadow a country's specific requirements for rule of law reform. Funds often follow the donor's mission rather than the needs of the recipient countries. If donor assistance is not recipient-driven, but is thrust upon a country, even ever so gently, ownership of the rule of law reform project and an assurance of its sustainability are tenuous.

Concurrent with an identification of a country's needs is the political will within the country to address the needs. Without it, foreign assistance fails completely, or, alternatively, takes an inordinate amount of time and resources to have an impact. In former communist countries, there was considerable political will for rule of law reform as many of these countries wanted to become members of the Council of Europe and/or NATO as well as accede to the European Union. These were powerful incentives that facilitated rule of law efforts. However, the donor's strategic interest in a country often blinds it to the lack of political will in the country. One could question whether there is political will for rule of law reform in Afghanistan, where hundreds of millions of dollars have been expended by the U.S. government to develop the formal and informal justice systems.

Ensuring there is political will in a country before genuine rule of law assistance is provided, initially requires a top-down approach. There must be realistic assurances from senior leadership within a country, that political will exists to support the financial and technical efforts of donors to implement rule of law reforms that address the country's specific needs which have been identified by the same leaders. Political will alone, however, is not sufficient if it is simply a verbal commitment. It must be accompanied with sufficient human resources throughout the justice system who are not only competent, but also have the appropriate authority to implement rule of law reforms. At this point, the bottom-up approach usually begins and can flourish. Yet, "One size doesn't fit all," stated a senior level Latvian judge. "The inception of rule of law work can either emanate from using the top-down or bottom-up approach, but in the end, there must be governmental political will."

With political will in place and human resources and professional authority in sufficient supply, donors will have a canvas upon which appropriate, sustaining rule of law programs can be developed. Under these circumstances, the role of the rule of law practitioner may be reduced significantly to providing expertise. In a rule of law program for which genuine results are anticipated, the practitioner does not need to, nor should engage in the actual work, but instead advise and guide local professionals to perform the work in order to guarantee local ownership of the reform. This is an extremely important factor in ensuring the sustainability of rule of law assistance.

It is tempting for rule of law practitioners to do the work themselves which, in some circumstances, is much easier and considerably faster. One of the major reasons for the slow process in working with beneficiaries is that, unlike in the U.S. where we focus on position and title rather than the person, in most countries it is crucial that trust exists in a relationship before essential work can be accomplished. Thus, it is not uncommon for a rule of law practitioner to attend several meetings with beneficiaries, before they will take concrete steps to support a rule of law project. Beneficiaries must first develop trust in the practitioner. Once that occurs, endless possibilities for fruitful cooperation can emerge. On a more cynical side, some practitioners engage in hands-on work as it helps with donor reporting requirements by showing quick results that can lead, at times, to increased funding.

Rule of law practitioners can achieve greater success with beneficiaries if their rule of law activities are visibly supported by senior level officials of the donor, particularly if the donor represents a government. A crucial element of the success of PIOR in Bulgaria and the LJTC in Latvia, is the public support demonstrated by U.S. Ambassador Bill Montgomery in Bulgaria and U.S. Ambassador Larry Napper in Latvia, as well as the USAID representative in each country. Their voices gave credibility to the creation of the judicial training assistance that was being provided and demonstrated to the beneficiaries the seriousness with which the U.S. government viewed such assistance.

Another example is the incomparable support U.S. Ambassador Al La Porta and the USAID mission director Ed Birgells provided in 2000 in developing the Five-Year Strategic Plan for the Justice System of Mongolia. While I was the rule of law consultant in Mongolia with the responsibility of creating the strategic process for justice sector professionals in Mongolia to draft their own justice sector plan, the success of the strategic process, including unanimous approval of the Strategic Plan by the Mongolian Parliament, is due primarily to the visible commitment by both officials to the strategic planning process. In addition to publicly supporting the Strategic Plan, they hosted a visit by Supreme Court Justice Sandra Day O'Connor to support the efforts of the Mongolian justice officials. All of these external efforts demonstrate that rule of law practitioners should not work in a vacuum if serious reform is anticipated.

While strong support within the echelon of a rule of law donor is critical, and while it is preferable to have more than one donor for fundamental rule of law assistance, a recurring problem in rule of law assistance is donor overload. It typically occurs as the result of donors focusing more on their own interests than that of the recipient country's needs.

A senior level Baltic judge recently assisted in a European Union Twinning project by working on a short-term assignment in a country teeming with donors. In his words, "There were 28 organizations working on the rule of law, yet they had different ideas of what the country needed. Their objectives were overlapping and there was weak coordination among themselves. Further, it appears that their activities were designed and planned according to the budget of the organization rather than the needs of the country. Their activities seemed so chaotic that one was led to believe these rule of law practitioners were engaging in work simply for the purpose of reporting."

A prime example of current donor overload is Kosovo, where rule of law practitioners from the U.S. and Europe are occupying several desks in the same ministries as well as other recipient institutions. The missions of the American and

European donors are disparate, resulting in overlapping and even competing rule of law activities. Without a doubt, there are strategic concerns that require these countries to have a physical presence as Kosovo is volatile. However, to ignore or not take seriously the mission and rule of law activities of each donor is inexcusable, particularly since the needs of Kosovo for democratic reform remain significant despite the considerable rule of law assistance Kosovo has received since 1999.

One senior official in the Kosovo Ministry of Justice stated, "Some of our laws look like sausage, as we have to accommodate the incongruent advice by donors whom we do not want to disappoint given their funding to the MOJ." Several local attorneys with whom I worked in other countries reported that their governments had to work hard to convince donors to "adjust their international assistance to meet the needs of the country rather than the priorities of the donors".

Funding is one of the major issues concerning effective rule of law assistance. While the financial assistance a country received in the early 90s is a pittance compared to today, it is questionable whether the return on today's massive investment in rule of law development justifies the effort.

Yet, regardless of the amounts of funding, several Bulgarian jurists believe that "donors should have concentrated on ensuring the success of a rule of law project rather than dispersing funds to a variety of projects, many of which, due to insufficient attention and resources, did not succeed. In Bulgaria, we witnessed the creation of several donor-funded projects that were *ab ovo*. Donors should also have focused on existing projects in Bulgaria ensuring their success and sustainability, rather than create similar projects, all with limited funding and duration, in other countries. A better methodology for rule of law assistance is to have local legal professionals, who have benefited from a successful and self-sustaining rule of law project transfer their knowledge and experience to neighboring countries, rather than rely only on international practitioners."

When many of us began our rule of law work in the early 90s, we believed, naïvely, that our work could accomplish the necessary results within a few years' time. Perhaps it was because we were fortunate to meet with such receptive legal professionals who were committed to democratic reforms, who were eager to work hard, still inspired by the unexpected demise of communism, and who, with little financial and technical assistance, took ownership of the reforms. We had common goals that were unfettered, we had an uncharted course that was receptive to ingenuity and tenacity, and we had a commitment to change that was not diminished by external bureaucratic factors. We agreed with Justice Sandra Day O'Connor, who told us that our job was to work ourselves out of a job, which many of us thought would be imminent.

While we initially thought we were building institutions, it has become clear that the real legacy for our rule of law work is the impact with the individuals with whom we worked. Several Latvian judges agreed with their colleague who stated, "while ABA ROLI and other donors helped to create the LJTC, one of the most rewarding aspects of their support was exposing Latvian judges and attorneys to the justice systems in other countries, by sending us to international conferences where we met our counterparts, who deeply understood our issues and with whom we could devise common solutions. Additionally, it was eye-opening to witness the professionalism of judges and attorneys in democratic countries who were our inspiration."

In the words of a Bulgarian judge, "The most important impact of rule of law assistance was the opportunity to look behind the iron curtain to a completely different governmental system that embraced democratic principles, and to think outside the box of communist ideology."

While the institutions we helped to create may not have become self-sustaining, we had an immense impact in transferring skills to our local counterparts who became leaders of the very institutions we tried to reform. Additionally, we helped to develop the capacity of individuals to replace American expertise and assume the responsibilities of enhancing the rule of law in their own countries.

In addition to the lawyers and judges with whom I worked in Bulgaria, Latvia, and numerous other countries who benefited from ABA ROLI assistance, several law students who were ABA ROLI staff have become prominent lawyers today. One young law student with whom I worked in Slovakia, became the Minister of Justice and later the Minister of Interior.

A Latvian law student with whom I worked wrote, "Rule-of-law practitioners gave us opportunities and opened a door for us. It was up to us to walk through that door and make it on our own. Without that door, I wouldn't be where I am today. What those rule of law practitioners did for us has become the credo of my life, and I am now opening the doors for others."

What is also gratifying are the rule of law projects today that are primarily run by local legal professionals, although funded by the U.S. government. A few years ago, I evaluated the USAID Access to Justice program in Ukraine, which was uniquely Ukrainian-staffed. The eight-person staff had developed the skills to take the helm and created a successful program of Ukrainian NGOs, student legal clinics, and law firms to ensure the underserved population in Ukraine had access to legal assistance. The only American expert involved in the program was U.S.-based. There is no better proof of our efforts in transferring skills to local leaders and ensuring the sustainability of rule of law programs.

Developing the rule of law in emerging democracies has been challenging and exhilarating. Working with intelligent, vibrant legal professionals, who are committed to democratic reforms in countries with varying degrees of political will, and often under circumstances where their job security is at risk, has been humbling. We rule of law practitioners can always return home, while our local counterparts remain in their country living with the consequences of our work together.

As I reflect upon the past 24 years, I realize that the richness of my life has not come from an income, nor from possessions, but from living my passion developing the rule of law in emerging democracies. It has come from the incalculable experiences I've had traveling the world, meeting with influential people who can and do make a difference in their country, discussing fundamental issues of democracy with foreign legal professionals, developing friendships with those whose experiences are vastly different from my own, yet embracing our similarities, and exploring vastly different cultures in countries most people only read about.

Mary Noel Pepys with Lebanese lawyers and judges.

Mary Noel Pepys with Kyrgyzstan judges.

Conclusion
Justice Joseph Nadeau

Most of the things worth doing in the world
had been declared impossible before they
were done.
Louis D. Brandeis – Associate Justice,
United States Supreme Court

A historic picture taken in 2004 at the newly established CEELI
Institute in Prague. Iraqi judges in attendance at the Institute's first
class; a two-week training program on Judging in a Democratic
Society.

Those of us who have worked internationally know that
change is not easy, that progress takes patience. Are we
discouraged from time to time? Sure. But it is also rewarding to
work with people of other nations who are trying to eradicate
corruption, to protect individual rights, and to enhance the
institutions of government.

There is no question that a fine balance is necessary to cultivate and maintain democratic principles. We should not expect that balance to come quickly or easily.

Let me cite a few ways USAID projects continue to excite me.

2005 – Bratislava, Slovakia – Judge Ludvik Bradac, Chairman of the local regional court, was our host at the Iraqi conference. On the first day of the conference, he asked me if I had participated ten years earlier in a regional workshop in Sofia, Bulgaria, attended by judges and government officials from Slovakia. When I told him I had, he left the room and returned quickly requesting that I talk to someone on his cell phone. The person on the line was an English-speaking judge who had attended that 1995 conference. For about five minutes, he proudly told me of the tremendous technological and management progress the Slovakian courts had made. That is USAID staying power.

1995 – Slovakia – we spent a great deal of effort to locate an overhead projector to display my transparencies. In 2005, judges there made presentations on USAID supplied laptops.

1996 – Warsaw, Poland – an American prosecutor and I gave presentations to judges from fifteen countries in the hall where the former Warsaw Pact nations met during the Cold War.

1999 – Czech Republic – ABA volunteers gathered in Prague where we worked with judges from Russia and Europe to create a new training institute and to prepare curriculum for judicial trainings there.

1999 – Yerevan, Armenia – young, new public defenders asked the program leader if I would debate an Armenian law lecturer on the importance of an adversarial criminal justice system.

2005 – Bratislava, Slovakia – at the last meeting of the Iraqi conference, one of the senior judges gave me his personal Islamic prayer beads as a token of respect and thanks for our work. It was very moving. From that, I learned to bring some special personal mementos, often pins in the shape of New Hampshire, to give to participants.

2008 – Indonesia – a judge in Banda Aceh showed a USAID worker an ethics outline he received from me at a training program the year before, eleven hundred miles away, in Jakarta.

2010 – Egypt – school children in Luxor read books with the USAID emblem on the cover; typed on USAID supplied computers; teachers smiled as their students sang to us in English.

Countries interested in moving toward more democratic institutions welcome, and can benefit from, assistance from other nations. Leaders of those countries have begun to recognize that an independent judiciary is not a threat to the other branches of government, but rather, can generate public trust, encourage business investment, and provide stability to government.

The investment our country makes in international work, like that supported by USAID, does not just benefit other countries. Our nation and other nations have public, business, and social interests that benefit from stable institutions. A stable world is a peaceful world. Governments may change, leaders rise and fall, but ideas endure. The people endure

From these authors, it seems clear that whenever we have worked with judges and leaders of other countries, we have always learned as much from them as we hope they have learned from us.

In short, we have always felt at home abroad.

Epilogue

The international landscape has changed dramatically since the completion of the above narrative. The United States, before January 2017, was generally acknowledged by most of the nations of the earth as the leader in the international community on issues of international trade, international finance, international security, and efforts to create a peaceful world. The former U.S. Secretary of Defense, James Mattis, summed up the situation with the comment:

> "The greatest gift the greatest generation [the generation during World War II and immediately thereafter] left us was the rules based postwar international order."

Brief Bios of Our Authors

James Apple

Dr. Apple was President of the International Judicial Academy. The Academy provides instruction on how judges and court personnel should function in a modern court system. It has hosted participants from Central and Eastern Europe, South America, Southeast Asia, and China. Among his duties at the Federal Judicial Center, Dr. Apple was responsible for directing the Center's international programs, including more than 50 seminars and conferences, and hundreds of briefings for judges and legal officials from 152 countries. He had worked with and advised judges, court administrators, and Ministry of Justice officials from developing countries around the world.

He had published numerous articles and lectured on judges, courts, and court administration at judicial training institutes and universities outside of the United States. Before coming to Washington in 1990, Dr. Apple was a practicing trial lawyer in the Commonwealth of Kentucky for 25 years. He is a Fellow of the American College of Trial Lawyers, a member of the American Law Institute, and had held the rank of Advocate with the American Board of Trial Advocates.

He had a B.A. with Honors in Philosophy degree from the University of Virginia, where he was Editor-in-Chief of the student daily newspaper, a J.D. degree from the University of Virginia Law School, where he was an editor of the Virginia Law Review, and a Master of Laws (LL.M.) in international and comparative law from the University of Edinburgh.

Sadly, Dr. Apple passed away before the publication of this book. He will be missed.

Thanaa Elshamy

Attorney Elshamy is an Egyptian lawyer and has served as Legal Consultant in the Ombudsman Office of the National Council of Women (NCW). She is an Access to Justice legal expert for the USAID-assisted Family Justice Program (FJP). She is Official Liaison Officer on behalf of FJP with Ministry of Justice and former legal adviser in the Ombudsman Office of the National Council of Women (NCW).

Bogdan Jędrys

Judge Jędrys presides in the Cracow Regional Court, Poland, handling serious criminal cases. He has participated in many international events organized by European Union entities, law faculties, or national magistrates' schools.

Mokhtar Lakhdari

Judge Lakhdari holds a diploma of judge from the Ecole Nationale d'Administration of Algiers (1986) and a Master in criminal law and criminology from the University of Algiers (2004). As general director of judiciary and legal affairs, Mr. Lakhdari was in charge of drafting laws, coordinating penal policy and promoting international judicial cooperation programs. From 2005 to 2015, he was the head of the criminal affairs and pardons direction in the ministry of justice and was directly involved in implementing counter terrorism laws and the Peace and Reconciliation Charter. He is a governmental Anti-Corruption expert for the review mechanism of the United Nation Convention Against Corruption. He participated in the negotiation of several bilateral mutual legal assistance treaties between Algeria and the United States, United Kingdom, France, Russian Federation, and Portugal. He has lectured at the judicial school and authored a book about the relationship between justice and media In January of 2018, he was appointed to the Supreme Court of Algeria.

Medhat Al-Mahmoud

Chief Justice Al-Mahmood was made minister for the Ministry of Justice by the Coalition Provisional Authority on 12 June 2003. In September 2003, when the independent Judicial Council was re-established (and the courts were removed from the Justice Ministry), he was appointed as the President. On 3 March 2005, he was appointed to the newly established constitutional court, the Federal Supreme Court (FSC), and unanimously elected by his fellow justices as its Chief Justice. After the transfer of sovereignty from the CPA, the Judicial Council was transformed into the Higher Judicial Council. By operation of law, the Chief Justice of the FSC is also the President of the Higher Judicial Council.

William Meyer

Attorney Meyer Bill served as the first liaison for the ABA's Central European and Eurasian Law Initiative (CEELI) in Sofia, Bulgaria. Since 1992, he has continued involvement in reform efforts in Russia, Ukraine, Lithuania, Armenia, Macedonia, Montenegro, Slovakia, Albania, Cambodia, Algeria, Bahrain, Egypt, Iraq, Jordan, Morocco, Syria, and Yemen. Bill was a founder of the International Legal Assistance Consortium based in Stockholm, Sweden. He was part of the American delegation selected by Supreme Court Justice Sandra Day O'Connor to participate in the sixteen-nation Arab Judicial Forum in Manama, Bahrain in 2003.

Justice Joseph Nadeau

Justice Nadeau is a graduate of Phillips Exeter Academy, and Dartmouth College. He received his J.D. from Boston University School of Law. He served on the New Hampshire Superior Court and was its Chief Justice until his appointment to the New Hampshire Supreme Court. He holds honorary Doctor of Law degrees from Southern New England School of Law and New England College. He received the Boston University School of Law Silver Shield Award in 2012. While serving as a judge and upon retirement, Justice Nadeau participated in National and regional Judicial Education projects in over twenty countries. Working with the Indonesian Supreme Court and USAID, he designed and participated in Judicial Performance and Code of Conduct education programs, training more than 2,000 Indonesian Judges.

Mary Noel Pepys

Attorney Pepys is a known international expert, specializing in international legal and judicial reform, for the past 23 years. She has lived and worked abroad in 41 countries including former communist countries, the Middle East, Asia, and Western Europe. She has worked with USAID, U.S. Department of State, The World Bank, United Nations Development Programme, and numerous U.S. contractors to provide legal and technical assistance to national governments, judiciary, bar, and law faculties. She has significant domestic governmental experience with local, state, and federal governments in the areas of diplomacy, peacekeeping, legislative drafting, judicial process, and governmental transparency.

Albert Scherr

Attorney Scherr is a professor of law at the University of New Hampshire School of Law & Chair of the International Criminal Law & Justice Program. Professor Scherr has extensive experience as a trial and appellate lawyer, and has handled over 40 homicide cases. He teaches courses in Criminal Procedure and Trial Advocacy. He also directs the Trial Advocacy Program at the law school. He has lectured to judges and lawyers on a variety of evidence issues in the United States and led a six-month training program in Russia.

Leigh Swigart

Dr. Leigh Swigart – Director of Programs in International Justice and Society at the International Center for Ethics, Justice, and Public Life of Brandeis University. She oversees the Brandeis Institute for International Judges, She co-authored *The International Judge: An Introduction to the Men and Women Who Decide the World's Cases* (2007, Brandeis

University Press and Oxford University Press). Her current research focuses on how the International Criminal Court is managing the challenges of accommodating African language speakers in its investigations, in the courtroom, and in its outreach programming. Dr. Swigart has wide experience in Senegal.

Simone Troller

Ms. Troller has more than 15 years of professional experience in human rights, justice, and development. She held various senior-level positions and has worked with the UN Assistance Mission to Afghanistan, the UN development program in the Pacific region, as a senior researcher for Human Rights Watch, as well as for the Organization for Security and Cooperation in Europe's presences in Tajikistan and Ukraine. She joined the Swiss Agency for Cooperation and Development in 2014, as a senior advisor on human rights and justice at its headquarters in Bern.

Mila Reynolds Brun

Ms. Brun works as National Program Officer at the Swiss Development Cooperation Office (SDC) in Bolivia, in charge of the governance domain. She has more than 20 years of professional experience in development programs in Latin America, including reform processes in the Constituent Assembly of Bolivia (2006–2009) and its Judicial System since 2013. She held senior-level positions in Swiss (SDC) and German Cooperation (GIZ), and has conducted evaluation missions and consultancies in Latin America and Southeast Asia, with the Swedish Cooperation, the World Bank, and the UN Office in Bolivia.

Markus Zimmer

Mr. Zimmer served as administrator of the U.S. District Court for Utah. He advises government officials on institutional rule of law-based reform, development, and modernization. Since 1992, he has counseled judicial and justice systems' leaders in 30 countries. With Ed.M. and Ed.D. degrees from

Harvard University, he was a Fulbright Scholar at the University of Zurich. He is founding President of the International Association for Court Administration and currently chairs its Advisory Council. He is also Executive Editor of the International Journal on Court Administration.

www.ingramcontent.com/pod-product-compliance
Lightning Source LLC
Chambersburg PA
CBHW040135270326
41927CB00019B/3386